ON
THE IMPORTANCE
OF
EDUCATING THE INFANT POOR,

FROM THE AGE OF EIGHTEEN MONTHS,
TO SEVEN YEARS.

CONTAINING AN ACCOUNT OF THE

SPITALFIELDS INFANT SCHOOL,

AND THE

NEW SYSTEM OF INSTRUCTION

THERE ADOPTED.

TO WHICH IS ADDED,

A REPLY TO THE STRICTURES OF DR. POLE, AND THOSE OF THE
EDINBURGH REVIEW, RESPECTING THE AUTHOR'S
MODE OF MANAGING THE CHILDREN.

BY S. WILDERSPIN,
Master of the above School.

SECOND EDITION,
WITH CONSIDERABLE ADDITIONS.

"Whoso shall receive one such little child in my
name receiveth me." Matt. xviii. 5.
"Take heed that ye despise not one of these little
ones." Matt. xviii. 10.

ENTERED AT STATIONERS' HALL.

LONDON:

PRINTED FOR W. SIMPKIN & R. MARSHALL,
Stationers' Hall Court, Ludgate Street, and Sold
by THE AUTHOR, at the Infant School,
Quaker Street, Spitalfields.

1824.
Goyder, Printer, 415, Strand.

CONTENTS.

	PAGE
INTRODUCTION	13
Rules to be observed by the Parents of Children admitted into the Spitalfields Infant School.	33
Rules for the Master and Mistress	37
On Order	ib.
A General Mode of Teaching the Alphabet, whereby 300 Children may say it in fifteen minutes	40
A Second Method of Teaching the Alphabet, both in Printing and Writing	43
A Plan for Teaching the Tables of Arithmetic by means of Inch Cubes of Wood	48
A Method of giving little Children bodily exercise, improving their minds, and pleasing them at the same time	50
Plan for Teaching Infant Children by the aid of pictures	57
Joseph's Dream	61
On the Formation of Character	84
On the Increase of Juvenile Delinquency	96
A number of Facts and Anecdotes	110
Play Ground	133
On Rewards and Punishments	139
On Cleanliness	159
Dimensions of a School-room capable of containing 300 Infant Children.	163
On the ill consequences of Frightening Children	165
On the Diseases of Children	169
Plan to prevent Accidents at School	173
On the dangers Children are exposed to between the ages of two and seven years	174
Qualifications of a Master and Mistress	195
Questions and Answers concerning the Geometrical Figures	202
Conclusion	209
APPENDIX	211

DEDICATION.

To

JOSEPH WILSON, Esquire,

OF BATTERSEA RISE,

This little Volume is humbly dedicated, in testimony of his exertions to establish Infant Schools, particularly the Infant School in Spitalfields.

SIR,

Living, as I do, in the neighbourhood of Spitalfields, I have a greater opportunity than you can have of witnessing the good effects of your philanthropy. Many of the parents could scarcely conceive it possible that any individual could be found, who would sacrifice so much, for their good and the good of their children, and I have been desired by them, to return their most grateful thanks. But, Sir, what are the thanks of the whole *world, compared to that holy flame, which Charity never fails to engender in the breast of that person who does good purely for its own sake. Divine providence always causes such good to be productive; and many persons who have visited your school, are so convinced of its utility, that they are about to establish similar Institutions, and these are persons of the first talent, and therefore not likely to be deceived; thus verifying that truth, which says, that from a small seed shall be produced a large tree, so that the fowls of the heavens may come and lodge in the branches thereof,*

That you, Sir, who have sacrificed a part of your fortune in this good work, may be returned tenfold, is the earnest wish of

THE AUTHOR.

PREFACE.

IN consequence of the rapid sale of the first edition of this work, I have been induced to reprint it, with such alterations as I think will give additional satisfaction. Many new facts, and much new information, will be found in this edition, all, I trust, tending to demonstrate the vast importance of early instruction. At the request of the reviewers, (who spoke favourably of the first edition) I have entered more into detail. Some of the information that will be found in it, I have obtained with great difficulty and personal hazard, by being obliged to mix with persons of the lowest description; and although this method of obtaining information must be considered as very disagreeable and a sacrifice of time, yet, in some instances, it is expedient to resort to it. Now although this little volume is presented to the Public in " a plain and unvarnished style," (as observed by my esteemed friend Mr. Lloyd, in his preface to the first edition,) yet I do conceive that it contains information which may be practically useful, the greater part of which being derived from practice itself. This, I really think, surpasses all theoretical views, for experience must ever be considered as the test of truth. I have endeavoured to establish and enforce the compatibility of sound religious instruction, with the rudimental education of the infant mind; and this, I hope, upon mature deliberation and reflection, will ever be found desirable. Many circumstances, as mentioned in the following pages, evidently show the utility of an early education, and particularly that of a religious kind. The improvement of the labouring classes of society has been, and will most assuredly be effected. How many parents have had to lament that their children have not been properly trained during their infancy: stubborness of disposition has often been the result of such neglect. But in addition to this, the vices that children of a very early age manifest, as exemplified in this work, is sufficient to create, in any feeling breast, a desire to rescue them from the power and influence of evil; and surely no way can prove more effectual to accomplish so desirable an end than the system which this work advocates and recommends. I have endeavoured to steer clear of the different theological prejudices, as professed by Christians of different denominations, conceiving that institutions of this kind ought to receive the support of all. What sort of religious doctrine and faith, therefore, the children ought to be taught I have not ventured to declare, as I consider it must be the wish and desire of all the disciples of Christ, that children should be taught the leading and fundamental truths, as made known in that source of eternal light, the everlasting Gospel. With these views, then, the following work, in its enlarged and (it is conceived) corrected form, is humbly submitted to the perusal of the christian reader, hoping that those who approve of what is therein contained, will use their endeavours to extend its circulation. The first edition was, by some persons, considered too high a price; in order therefore to meet the views of such, I shall continue the same price, although there is twice as much information contained in this second edition. Trusting that He who is Life Itself, will prosper this further endeavour to the extension of His own glory among men, I shall now leave it to the consideration of the judicious and considerate reader, and that he may smile with complacency on this (I hope) well-meant endeavour, is the sincere wish of

THE AUTHOR.

INTRODUCTION.

IT has long been a subject of deep regret to many pious and well disposed persons that, notwithstanding the numerous charitable institutions which abound in this country, our prisons should still remain crowded; and although there is an increase in the police establishment, and much vigilence exercised by the Magistracy, that still crimes of every description should rather increase than diminish. The good that has been done by the Bible Societies, School Societies, and Institutions of a similar nature, is, perhaps, incalculable; and were it not for these excellent Institutions, there is no doubt but that crimes would be still more numerous than they are. Probably one reason that may be assigned for the increase of crime, is the increase of population, and another poverty; and I think there is not any thing better calculated to prevent this evil, than taking the children of the poor out of the streets; for there, it must be acknowledged, they can learn no good, but much evil. How many children, ere they can lisp their own name, will learn to steal and pilfer; I wish I could say I had never been an eye-witness to the fact; but I have been, in many instances. What is a poor woman to do, if left a widow, with four or five children, the eldest perhaps not more than ten years of age? She is obliged to go out to her daily labour, and the consequence is, that her children are left to shift for themselves, because the mother is not able to pay for their schooling. The Free Schools will not admit them because they are too young; and thus they imbibe principles and habits, of which neither parents, tutors, nor even the law itself, in many instances, can ever break them.

It is an old proverb—"*bend the twig while it is young;*" and it is our duty both in a civil, moral, and religious point of view, to take particular care of the infant mind. Great and many are the dangers that children are exposed to, between the ages of two and seven years; for when they have been successful in stealing an orange, or an apple, they will not stop there, but make a second attempt, and it is not unlikely but that they will get so confirmed in evil, before they are seven years old, as to prefer the street to the school, or any useful employment. This, then, is a very great evil, but is not all: not a week passes, but we read in the public papers, of little children being run over by coaches, or other vehicles; or of their being burnt to death, in consequence of being left alone.

Should any person still ask what can be the utility of taking children out of the streets so very young, I would answer, that it is likely to prove one of the greatest preventatives of crime that has been thought of for the last century. In confirmation of this assertion, I would state, that all instruction is, and must be, received in a state of humility. This can be proved by every day's experience. For example, take a person who has confirmed himself in any particular opinion, and thereby conceives he knows much, and we shall find him a very stubborn pupil. However erroneous such opinion may be, he will defend it with all his might. Nay, I was told by an old thief, that he had as much right to live as any body else; that thieving was his profession, and that he should follow it. I could plainly perceive, from the conversation I had with him, that he had confirmed himself in an opinion, that thieving was no harm, providing he used no violence to the person of any one. He seemed to have no idea of the rights of property, and consequently thought himself justified, (as he had no property of his own) to prey upon the property of others. That it is difficult to reclaim a child that has once been associated with thieves, may be gathered from the following case:

"Richard Leworthy, aged fourteen, was indicted for stealing five sovereigns, the property of William Newling, his master.

"The prosecutor stated, that he resided in the Commercial-road, and is by business a tailor—the prisoner had been his apprentice for four months, up to the 28th of August, when he committed the robbery—on that day he gave him five pounds to take to Mr. Wells, of Bishopsgate Street, to discharge a bill—he never went, nor did he return home—did not hear of him for three weeks, when he found him at Windsor, and apprehended him. He admitted having applied the money to his own use—he was found at a public house—he said he had spent all his money except one shilling and six pence.

"A shopman in the service of Mr. Wells stated, that in August last the witness owed his master a sum of money—knew the prisoner—he did not bring money to their shop, either on or since the 28th of August.

"The prisoner made no defence, but called his master, who said he received him from the Refuge for the Destitute, and received a good character with him. He would not take him back again.

"Mr. Wontner stated, that he had received two communications from the Rev. Mr. Crosby, the Chaplain of the Institution, stating they would not interfere on his behalf.

"The Jury returned a verdict of *Guilty*.

"Mr. Justice Park observed, that the best course would be to send him out of the country."

Here we see that, notwithstanding all the pious instructions and well meant endeavours of the conductors of the Refuge for the Destitute, the boy was only four months in his master's employ, before he falls into his old habits; and the conductors of the Refuge were so convinced that the boy was so confirmed in such practices, that they refused to have any thing more to do with him. This is one instance, to show the propriety of early instruction, not in letters merely, but in principles of virtue and honesty. If a child was ever so well inclined, and yet allowed to associate with evil disposed persons, he would insensibly fall into their way of life. This may be seen from the following circumstance.

"Captain Edwardson, of the Snapper, brings from New Zealand two chiefs, one of whom is accompanied by his wife. One of them is a youth of about sixteen; and the other is thirty years old. The name of the latter is James Caddel, an Englishman by birth, and whose history is briefly as follows: In 1807, or thereabouts, the ship Sydney Cove, a sealer, out of this port, was cruizing off the Bay of Islands, and had either stationed or despatched a boat's crew, consisting of five hands and a boy, (James Caddel, the present chief,) to one of the islands in quest of seals. The boat was taken by the savages in the vicinity of the southern Cape, and the helpless men, with the exception of Caddel, were killed and eaten. Fortunately, in his fright, the boy flew to an old chief for mercy, and happened to touch his *ka-kah-how*, (the outward mat of the chief,) and thus his life became preserved, as his person was then held sacred. Being in too distant a part of New Zealand to indulge the hope of hastily escaping from a wretched captivity, Caddel became resigned to his apparent destiny, and insensibly adopted the manners and customs of the natives. About nine years since he was allied to a chief's daughter, who also is sister to a chief; and, by this two-fold tie, he became a prince of no small influence among such subjects as those barbarous despots are destined, in the present constitution of things, to have the control of. Caddel lost his own language, as well as European customs, and soon became transformed from the English sailor-boy, into the dauntless and terrifying New Zealand Chief. It required some argumentation to induce him to visit New South Wales; and he would not have come without his partner, to whom he appears to be tenderly attached."

This is just the case with all children, they would learn any language, adopt any manners and customs, be they bad or good, and therefore I consider it to be of public importance, in every point of view, to take children out of harm's way, as soon as they can walk. No better plan could be devised in my opinion, for the improvement and comfort of slaves in the West Indies, and other of his Majesty's colonies, than by establishing infant schools for the instruction of their children. They might be taught to speak as we do in this country, and instructed, I think, with as great care as our own children; this would produce a great change for the better, it would be gradual, and consequently not dangerous, for all sudden changes are pregnant with danger, but this would be free from that objection, and therefore the more desirable. Early impressions made in the infant minds of the sable sons of Africa, would be likely to prove of more benefit to them, to us, and to their sovereign, than at first view we might be inclined to believe. Many facts will be found in this work to prove the early depravity of children; and as many might be produced to show that the contrary would be the case, if proper care was taken of them. At a late public meeting, a gentleman stated, that it was too soon to begin with children at such an early age; observing, likewise, that it was not usual to begin to sow seed before sun-rise. I know no reason why seed should not be sown before sun-rise; nor do I know that it would prove detrimental to the seed by being sown thus early: but this I do know, that the seeds of vice are very early nourished in the infant mind, and if the seeds of vice will fructify in the infant mind, it is not too much to expect that the seeds of virtue, if sown, will do the same. The gentleman further stated, that the parents had a right to take care of their own children; this must be admitted: but do they? We see that many of them will not take care of themselves; and when this is the case they will be sure to neglect their children. It will be seen in this book, that many parents are not able to take care of their children, if they were ever so well disposed; and if this is the only argument that can be brought forward against Infant Schools, I shall not fear their becoming universal. I have mentioned several cases of juvenile depravity, where I have treated on that subject, but as an additional proof of the utility of Infant Schools, I will insert one more, which, probably, will scarely be credited; and had it not been for the spirited conduct of an individual, who mustered sufficient courage to prosecute the offender, the case would have been buried in oblivion, like hundreds of others.

"William Hart, an urchin, seven years of age, was indicted for stealing twenty-two shillings in money, numbered, from the person of Mary Connor.

"The prosecutrix stated, that on the day named in the indictment, she took twenty-five shillings to get something out of pledge, but as there was a crowd in Mary-le-bone assembled, to witness a fight, she was induced to join the mob—while standing there, she felt something move in her pocket, and putting her hand outside her clothes, and laid hold of what proved to be the hand of the prisoner, which she held until she had given him a slap of the face, and then she let him go—she felt in her pocket, and discovered that only three shillings were left; here a constable took him up, and accused him of robbing her of twenty-two shillings—the prisoner said, I have twenty-two shillings in my pocket, but it is my mother's, she gets so drunk she gives it me to take care of.

"The officer stated to the same effect, and

added that, in a secret pocket in his jacket, he found fourteen shillings and six-pence. It was the practice of gangs of pickpockets to have a child like this to commit the robbery, and hand the plunder to them. Witness went to his parents, who said he had been absent seven weeks, and they would have nothing to do with him.

"Mr. Baron Garrow, in feeling terms, lamented that a child of such tender years should be so depraved. He added—"I suppose, gentlemen, I need only ask you to deliver your verdict.

"His Lordship then observed that he would consult his learned brother, as to the manner the prisoner should be disposed of. They at length decided that, although it might seem harsh, the Court would record against him fourteen years' transportation; and no doubt but government would place him in some school, where, if he behaved well, it would not be carried into full effect."

This will be found exactly to coincide with what I have stated in other parts of this work; and surely, with such facts before our eyes, it must be obvious, that infant schools have not been thought of a moment too soon.

It may now be proper for me to show to whom the public are indebted, for the establishment of the first Infant School. I do not know with whom the idea first origi-

INTRODUCTION. 23

nated, nor do I think it is of much importance to know this; the point is, who first brought it into action? The first Infant School that we heard of in this country, was established at Westminster, in the year 1819; the master of that Institution is, J. Buchanan, who came from Mr. Owen's Establishment, at New Lanark, where an Infant School had been previously formed by that gentleman; the gentlemen who established the school at Westminster, were the following:—Henry Brougham, Esq. M.P.; James Mill, Esq. John Smith, M.P. The Marquis of Lansdowne; Zacariah Macauly, Esq. Thomas Babington, Esq. Lord Dacre; Sir Thomas Baring; William Leake, M. P. Henry Hase, Esq. Benjamin Smith; John Walker, Esq. and Joseph Wilson, Esq. The latter gentleman was so convinced of the importance of Infant schools, that he soon afterwards established one at his own expense; and the success that has attended the plan that is there pursued, is fully stated in this book. Soon after this there were Infant Schools established at the following places, viz. at Islington, White Chapel, Brampton, in Huntingdonshire, Blackfriars, (Putney), Bristol, Worthing, Liverpool, and Wandsworth. The Reverend William Wilson, Vicar of Walthamstow, Essex, brother to Mr. Joseph Wilson, is about establishing one at Walthamstow; and at Lady-day next there will be one opened by some gentlemen, in the parish of St. Luke's, Middlesex, capable of accommodating seven hundred infants; so that the public will soon have an opportunity of witnessing the great importance of Infant Schools, and of their tendency to prevent every species of crime. They will see that it is no visionary scheme, but a thing that deserves the support of all Christians. There is another argument in favour of Infant Schools, which is, that they will form an asylum for blind or deaf children. We have two of the former, a boy and girl, and we find them no more trouble than any of the others; they learn the hymns, the pence and multiplication tables, and every thing the same as the other children, except letters and reading, and who are delighted to be noticed by, and play with the other children. As children are so apt to imitate, I have no doubt that deaf children would be delighted to see the performances of the other children, and quickly imitate them. I am almost confirmed in this opinion by the conversation I had with Mr. Arrowsmith, brother to the artist of that name. He says, that deaf and dumb children will learn quicker with other children that can hear, than they would with children like themselves; and I am inclined to favour his opinion, because we teach a great deal by means of the eye. It is a current remark, that deaf and dumb children are very mischievous; and, indeed, how can we expect it otherwise, when they are treated as outcasts by most other children; but if they were sent to school with other children, I think this would not be the case; at all events, I will take, (with Mr. Wilson's permission,) all such children whose parents apply for their admission.

There is one objection I understand which has been made against Infant Schools, and that is, that it is taking the work out of the parents hands, and it is considered that it will lull the parents into a false security, by depending upon other persons to do that for their children which they were in duty bound to do for them themselves; this objection will apply to all free schools, and consequently should have been made before, for it is as much the duty of parents to take care of their children after they are six years of age, as it is to take care of them before that age; and it is forcibly impressed upon my mind, that if we wait until the poor are qualified and willing to educate their children, we shall wait a considerable time. In another part of this work I have given a few hints on the subject of the parents paying for the care and education of their children, and have prepared a method by which every one should be made to bear a part of the expences of these Institutions; indeed I am persuaded that if government would sanction this plan of teaching infants merely by building the schools, that the money for the other expenses of carrying on the schools would be made up by the parents, with the aid of charitable individuals, but to carry them on upon a sure and permanent footing, I think the plan I have recommended in page 186 to be preferable.

Another objection has been made to Infant Schools, viz. It was thought that they would tend to encourage the poor to marry, without considering whether they possessed the means of supporting their offspring. From what I know of the poor, I am inclined to believe that Infant Schools would have very little influence upon them in that respect; for while they continue to be human beings, and continue to possess the same feelings and inclinations, that all human beings are subject to, they will most certainly continue to marry, and whatever miseries have been entailed upon the poor, and society at large, by early marriages, the miseries that have been entailed upon them, and society, by the opposite life, is not to be compared therewith. Hence I conceive that this objection is of little weight as there are, and perhaps always will be a great number of poor children in the world, therefore it behoves us to endeavour to make them as happy as we can and as useful to society as possible.

It is well known that, by nature, we are too apt to bend towards evil, rather than towards good; that we are too apt to imbibe bad principles, rather than good ones; hence the greatest care is necessary to be taken with children, at the time when they receive their first impressions. The children of the rich have every possible care taken of them, being seldom, or never left alone, and never suffered to go into the streets without a guide; and consequently, should any evil manifest itself, it is immediately detected; but it is not so with the children of the poor, for they are surrounded by every kind of danger and temptation.

It is not along since I read in the Police Reports, of a woman who had entrapped eight or ten children from their parents, and had trained them up, and sent them out thieving; and it was not till one of the children was taken in the act of stealing, that the whole affair was made known. Had these children been taken care of, this woman would not have had an opportunity of enticing them away: and how do we know how many hundreds of children have been enticed away, under a promise of giving them merely a few cakes, or some other trifling reward.

This is by no means a solitary instance, for from the information I possess, I am convinced that a volume might be written on this subject; hence I conceive that Infant Schools are calculated to produce great national benefit; First, as tending to prevent the increase of crime, and likewise the loss of human life, by preventing, in a great measure, the numerous accidents that daily happen to children.*

Secondly, I presume that they will prove beneficial both to National and British Schools, and also Sunday Schools, throughout the kingdom, by depriving the parents of that common excuse for non-attendance

---

* Dr Pole mentions, in his observations on Infant Schools, page 17, "that in the year 1819, in London only, the number of boys who procured a considerable part of their subsistance by pocket picking, and thieving in every possible form, was estimated to be eleven to fifteen hundred. And he mentions one man in Wentworth Street, near Spitalfields, who had forty boys in training to steal and pick pockets, and who were paid by a part of their plunder: happily this man was convicted of theft and transported. This cirumstance, with many others, led to the establishment of a Sunday School in the neighbourhood. The Teachers and Superintendents, when seeking for scholars, found many parents living together in an unmarried state, and, by persuasion and encouragement, succeeded in getting three couple married the first quarter. Had these children been placed under the proper management of an Infant School, there is the fairest ground to presume, that little of the evil complained of would have happened; whereas the want of it has deprived many parents of their children, who, under a proper course of instruction, might have been a solace, comfort, and support in their declining years.

viz. "I was obliged to keep him at home to mind his little brother."

Thirdly, I am convinced, that it confers a benefit both on the children and parents: many of the latter freely acknowledge it; and I trust that Infant Schools will tend to verify that portion of Scripture, which says, "*Train up a child in the way he should go, and when he is old he will not depart from it.*" Although this seems not to be the case in all instances, still we are quite certain that if good seed is never sown, it can never spring up; for the minds of children, and indeed of men, may very justly be compared to a garden, which, if not attended to, will be soon over-run with all kinds of noxious weeds, which will take such root as frequently to choke every good thought and affection, and even conscience itself.

Lastly, every argument that can be brought forward in support of education in general, and the National and British systems in particular, may be brought forward in support of Infant Schools, with this additional weight, that infancy is the time in which we receive our first impressions, and if those impressions are bad, they are not easily effaced. We find that little children were the particular objects of our Divine Master's care, when he was on earth, as we thus read in the Gospel:—
"*And they brought unto him little children,*

that he should touch them; but the disciples rebuked those that brought them: but Jesus, beholding, was much displeased, and said, Suffer little children to come unto me, and forbid them not; for of such is the kingdom of heaven: and taking them up in his arms, and putting his hands upon them, he blessed them," Mark x. 13 to 16.

The Infant School in Quaker Street, Spitalfields, was opened July the 24th, 1820, and twenty-six children were admitted the first day; the next day twenty-one; on the 31st sixty-five, and on the 7th of August, thirty-eight; at which last date I and my wife were engaged by Joseph Wilson. Esq. to take the management thereof. This gentleman built the school-room, and supplied every thing necessary, at his own expence, and settled our salary.

Thus situated, we commenced, and soon found that we had a complete desert, as it were, to cultivate; for the children were mostly strangers to each other, and few of them knew their letters. The first thing that appeared necessary, was to form the children into classes, which being done, we endeavoured to select two children out of each class to act as monitors: but finding that there were not more than six children in the whole school that knew their letters, it was impossible to derive any assitance from them, in the way of teaching the others. The consequence was, we were obliged to take the children by one class at a time, and having supplied each child with a card, on which the alphabet was printed in large letters, we formed them into a square, and commenced by calling out A, and likewise desiring each child to point with his finger to the letter, which being done, the next letter was called, and so on, till the whole alphabet was repeated. By pursuing this plan, in course of time, we were enabled to find monitors who knew their letters, and by these means adopted a regular system, an account of which will be laid before the reader in the following pages.

ON INFANT EDUCATION.

Rules to be observed by the Parents of Children admitted into the Spitalfields Infant School.

1.

PARENTS are to send their children clean washed, with their hair cut short and combed, and their clothes well mended, by half past eight o'clock in the morning, to remain till twelve.

2.

If any child be later in attendance than nine o'clock in the morning, that child must be sent back until the afternoon; and in case of being later than two in the afternoon, it will be sent back for the day.

3.

Parents may send their children's dinners with them in the morning, so that they may be taken care of the whole day, to enable the mother to go out to work.

4.

If a child be absent, without notice being sent to the master or mistress, assigning a satisfactory reason for the absence, such child will not be permitted to return again to the school.

Saturday afternoon is half-holiday.

※※※ It is earnestly hoped, that parents will see their own interest, as well as that of their children, in strictly observing the above rules; and they are exhorted to submit to their children being governed by the master and mistress; to give them good instruction and advice; to accustom them to family prayer; but particularly to see that they repeat the Lord's prayer, when they rise in the morning, and when they retire to rest, and set before them a good example; for in so doing they may humbly hope that the blessing of Almighty God will rest upon them and their families; for we are assured in the holy Scriptures, that if we train up a child in the way he should go, that when he is old he will not depart from it, *Prov.* xxii. 6. Therefore you may be instrumental in the promotion of their welfare in this life, and of their eternal happiness in the world to come.

On each of these Rules I shall make a few remarks.

First. The reader will see the utility of this rule at first sight, for some parents are so naturally dirty, that they would not wash their children from one week's end to another, unless required so to do, and if it was to be done for them, they would not be so thankful as when compelled to do it themselves; this I have experienced to be the fact.

Second. With respect to this rule, it has

its advantages, for it would not be right to punish the children when the fault rested with their parents, consequently by sending them home, the real authors of the mischief get punished; for many of the parents have told me, that when their children have been at home, they employed themselves in singing the alphabet, or counting, patting their hands, &c. &c. that it was impossible to keep an infant a sleep, and that they were glad to get them out of the way, and have said they would take care that their children should not be late again.

But as there is no rule without an exception, so I have found that this rule has its disadvantages, for some of the elder children would, when they wanted a half-holiday, take care to be late, in order to find the door shut, although they were sent in proper time by their parents; this, when detected, subjects them to a pat on the hand, which is the only corporeal punishment we have. If this rule were not strictly enforced, the children would be coming at all hours of the day, which would put the school into such disorder, that we should never know when all the children had said their lessons.

Third. This rule is of great service to those parents who go out to work; for by sending the children's dinners with them, they are enabled to do their work in comfort;

and the children, when properly disciplined, will be no additional trouble to the teacher, for they will play about the play-ground, while he gets his dinner, without doing the least mischief.

Fourth. This rule also has its uses, for many persons will keep their children away for a month or two, when nothing is the matter with them, consequently the children will lose almost all they have learned at school: besides it keeps a child out, who perhaps would attend regularly, and we should never know how many children were in the establishment; therefore if a parent does not attend to this rule, the child's name is struck off the book.

On the admission of a child into the school, the parents are supplied with a copy of the above rules, and this prevents them from pleading any excuse; the rules are fastened on pasteboard, otherwise the parents would double them up and put them into their pockets, and forget all about them: but being on pasteboard, the parents hang them up in their dwellings.

The short exhortation that follows, it is hoped, may have its uses, by reminding the parents of their duty, and thereby causing them to co-operate with those persons who have the welfare both of themselves and their children at heart.

Rules for the Master and Mistress.

1st. Never to correct a child in anger.

2nd. Never to deprive a child of any thing without returning it again.

3rd. Never to break a promise.

4th. Never to overlook a fault; but in all things study to set before the children an example worthy of imitation, that they may see your good works, and glorify your father which is in heaven.

On Order.

AS nothing can be done well without attention to order, so it is necessary that children, however young, should have some idea of it. Therefore on opening the school, I cause all the children to stand up, at a word of command, in an orderly manner; after which they all kneel down, when one of the children repeats a short prayer, and concludes with the Lord's prayer, the other children repeating it after him. After which, the boy who repeated the prayer gives out a hymn, and the children all sing it. It is pleasing to see how the little creatures will try to sing and keep time; indeed children generally seem to be very fond of singing, and therefore we teach them to sing the alphabet, to a tune, [Georges] which they do extremely well; likewise the pence and multiplication tables, which they soon learn. The hymn being concluded, they then commence their lessons, which they do in the following order:—

The school is divided into classes; there are two monitors appointed to each class; tins are fixed round the school with cards in them, from No. 1 up to No. 16, the same as are used in National Schools; one of the monitors then takes the children up to the cards, one at a time, the other monitor keeping the class in order while the lessons are going on. When the monitor, who first began, has finished half the class, the other one succeeds him, and teaches the remainder, the former monitor taking his place, so that the monitors share the work equally between them. No monitor is above seven years of age.

There is also a general monitor, whose business it is to walk round the school, and see that the monitors do their duty, and put the children's fingers to every letter or word according to what they are learning. In this manner they go on until every child in the school has said one lesson.

The class that has done first is taken into a separate room, where the children have each another lesson, though in a different way from the first, for in what we call the class room, each child is furnished with a card and tin, and being formed into a square, the whole class say their lessons together. For instance, one child leads off, the others following him, each keeping his finger to the word, whilst the teacher walks behind them, so that if any child is inattentive, he is sure of being detected.* It is not often that they are inattentive, for as it is an entire change of scene to what it was in the large room, the children generally like it, and consequently seldom look off their lessons. The lessons generally consist of about one hundred words, and it is astonishing how soon they will get through it, for by spelling all together it is a kind of play for them, and has this advantage, that it corrects bad pronunciation; for if a child pronounces his words incorrectly, (and it is seldom that two children, who pronounce wrong, will stand together,) therefore the children on each side of him, spelling right, he cannot avoid hearing them, and will try to imitate them, and of course get rid of his bad pronunciation; when the lesson is finished, they walk out of the room two and two, and another class succeeds them, who go through the same dicipline as above described.

* This part of the plan is not my own, but was taught me by the Master of the Westminster Infant School.

A General Mode of teaching the Alphabet, whereby 300 *Children may say it in fifteen Minutes.*

AS the human mind is formed for an endless variety, the oftner the scene can be changed the better, especially for children; for if little children are kept too long at one thing, they become disgusted and weary of it, and then their minds are not in a fit state to receive instruction. I cannot help thinking, that many persons, in their over anxiety to bring children forward in their learning, actually defeat their own intentions, by keeping the mind too constantly fixed upon one object. Where can be the utility of keeping a number of little children sitting in one position, for hours after they have said their lessons, and not suffering them to speak or exchange an idea with each other? No better way, in my humble opinion, can be taken to stupify them than such a mode; for little children are naturally lively, and if they are not suffered to move, but kept constantly in one position, they not only become disgusted with their lessons, but likewise with the school. Hence, perhaps, is one of the reasons why so many children cry on going to school; but as one of the principal ends in view, in *Infant Schools,* is to make the children happy, as well as to instruct them, so it is thought expedient to change the scene as often as possible.

The method of teaching that I am now about to describe is as follows, viz.:—The children are taught to stand in files, the smaller children, such as those from eighteen months to three years old, standing in front, the taller children standing behind; the alphabet is pasted on cards in two different characters, thus (a A) on one side of the card, and (b B) on the other side. The card is then put on the end of a stick, which is held up before all the children, who immediately call out A: one of the children then enquires how many there are, and the other children answer two: the stick is then turned round in the hand, and (b B) are exhibited, when one of the children enquires what letters they are, the other children answering as before: in this way we go on until we have gone through the whole of the alphabet.

They are also taught natural history in the same way, by placing pictures of birds and beasts at the end of the stick, and the children very soon learn the names of the different kinds of animals. To keep the children's attention fixed, and cause them to look at what we mean to put on the stick, we sometimes put the picture of a bird, or other animal, between the letters, which has a very good effect, for it not only changes the scene, but forms an agreable variety, and makes them more attentive. They never know what is about to be put upon the stick, for if they did, their attention would not be sufficiently arrested, and would, I think, look another way. The reader will perceive the utility of the above plan, as it not only fixes the children's attention, but teaches them two distinct alphabets, and natural history, at the same time.* In this way three or four hundred children may be taught, not only the alphabet and natural history, but spelling also; for by having a frame made about eighteen inches by twelve, with a socket to receive a common mop handle, and stuffed similar to the large frame described a little farther on, the brass letters may be stuck on it, and held up before all the children, when any word may be formed that suits their capacities. It is also to be observed, that a transparency might be used with very good effect, particularly on dark days and winter evenings, as that would tend to form that variety so necessary for children. Having finished a lesson of this description, they are permitted to go out into the play-

* The questions put to the children, when a picture is exhibited, will be found under the article, " Plan for teaching by the aid of pictures."

ground and divert themselves; but even there they learn lessons, such as the pence table, multiplication table, &c. of which more will be said when we come to treat of that part of the system.

A Second method of Teaching the Alphabet, both in Printing and Writing.

THE first method, as above described, is adapted for the large room, where the children may be taught altogether; but it is necessary to change the scene even in this, for however novel and pleasing a thing may be at first, if it is not managed with prudence it will lose half of its effect. But it is to be observed, that the last mode of teaching, described in the preceding article, is not practised every day, but only twice or thrice a week, and indeed the children will take care that the teacher does not forget to teach them, in any way that they have been accustomed to; for I generally teach them at their own request, and by letting the above plan lay by for a day or two, some of the children will come to me and say, "Please sir may we say the letters on the stick?" When some of the other children over-hearing that child ask the question, it will go through the school like lightning: " O yes—yes—yes sir, if you please, do let us say the letters on the stick:" thus a desire is created in the children's minds, and it is then that they may be taught with good effect.

The plan that I am about to describe is in practice almost every day, and is better adapted for what is called the class-room, and is taught thus:—we have the alphabet printed in large letters, both in roman and italic characters, on one sheet of paper; this paper is pasted on a board, or on pasteboard, and placed against the wall; the whole class then stand around it, but instead of one of the monitors pointing to the letters, the master or mistress does it; so that the children not only get instruction from each other, but every child has a lesson from the master or mistress twice every day.

It may be proper here to mention, that two persons are necessary to manage an infant school, a master and mistress, one being occupied in the large room, the other in the class room. The business of the person in the large room is to keep order, and to see that the monitors do their duty, and that the children do not look off their lessons; and the business of the master in the class-room is to teach the children himself: if in the alphabet, in the way above described, but if in spelling, each child is supplied with a card and tin, and they are taught as described in the section on order, in a former part of this work. The reason why the children are not taught spelling in the same way, is, because they are taught so by each other in the large room; and it is necessary to vary the scene, because it pleases the children, and they come to it with greater delight.

Raised letters might also be placed against the wall, put on ledges, or hung on nails: you might then tell any child in the class to fetch a certain letter, and if he did not bring the right one, the next child to him might go for it, and so on progressively, until they had brought every letter. This would please the children, and create emulation, and the novelty of the thing, if they did not have too much of it, would arrest their attention, and by that means, much might be done. The raised letters, if made of brass, would last for many years.*

The following plan has been adopted since the publication of the first edition, which has been found to answer very well. A frame should be made 3 feet square, of inch and half deal; on each side of this deal nail a piece of green baise, leaving room to stuff it with hay; when stuffed, let it be

* Brass letters cost from 2d. to 9d. each, according to size. I shall be happy to order them, of the maker, for any friends who may wish to purchase them.

quilted like a mattress, and fixed against the wall, in this the brass letters are to be stuck.

The expence of this article need not exceed 10 shillings. Persons in the country wishing to establish Infant Schools, may have brass letters and pictures, both of natural and scripture history, with every other necessary requisite for an Infant School, sent to them, by sending an order to the Master of the Spitalfields Infant School, accompanied with a remittance, or reference to some house in London for payment.

The method of teaching the writing Alphabet is as follows; the children that are about five years old are supplied with slates, on which is engraved the whole alphabet, the same as on copper-plate copies, thirteen letters on each side of the slate, some in capital letters others in text; the children then put the pencil into the engraving, and work it round into the shape of the letter, which they cannot avoid doing, as the pencil will keep in the engraved part; in this way they not only learn to read writing, but learn to form their letters very well, which may be seen by any person who pleases to visit the school. They are taught to make figures by the same method, and are also instructed in the two first rules of arithmetic by means of raised figures placed on the frame as follows; suppose the figure 5 is stuck at the bottom of the frame and one class of children standing opposite to it, the teacher will then enquire what figure it is ; some of the children will answer five ; if none of them know it, (which will be the case at first,) they must of course be told. Then place the figure 3 over the 5 and ask what the last figure is, and if the children answer correctly, then ask them how many are 3 and 5. Their having answered this question, place another figure over the 3, the figure 6 for example, enquire as before, what figure it is, and then, how many are eight and six when added together; and so on progressively as the teacher may think proper.

To assist the understanding and to exercise the judgment, in teaching numeration, stick a figure in the cushion, say figure 8. Question ; what is this? Answer ; No. 8, Q. If No. 1 be put on the left side of the 8 what will it be? A. 18 ; Q. If the 1 be put on the right side, then what will it be? A. 81. Q. If the figure 4 be put behind the 1, then what will the number be? A. 814. Shift the figure 4, and put it on the left side of the 8, then ask the children to tell the number, the answer is 481. The teacher can keep adding and shifting as he pleases, according to the capacity of his pupils, taking care to explain as he goes on, and to satisfy himself that his little flock perfectly understands him ; in this way the children are both pleased and edified, and it is very seldom out of from 180 to 200 children, (that being our usual compliment in attendance,) that any one is found crying.

A Plan for teaching the Tables of Arithmetic by means of Inch Cubes of Wood.

THIS plan, like the former, is best adapted for teaching children in classes, in the class room, because it would be difficult for all the children to get sight of the cubes, if the whole were taught together. The children are formed into a square in the class room, in the centre of which is placed a table; on this table the cubes are placed, one, two, or three at a time, according to the knowledge of the children: for example, the master puts down three, he enquires of the children how many there are, the children, seeing three on the table naturally call out three; the master will put down two more, and enquire as before, how many are three and two, they will answer five; put five more, and ask how many they make; perhaps some of the children will answer right, and others wrong; call those that answer wrong to the table, and let them count the cubes, one at a time, until they are correct, then add more to those on the table as far as the teacher thinks proper, say, for example, as far as eighty: the teacher may ask his little pupils how many tens there are in eighty, taking care to place the cubes ten in a row; the children seeing eight rows will most likely say eight: then ask them how many are eight times ten; the children will answer eighty: they may be cross examined in this way with good effect, until they begin to be tired, which as soon as the teacher perceives, he must begin to subtract, saying, take 2 from 80 how many remains? Answer 78. Q. take 8 from 78 how many remains? A. 70. The teacher may vary his questions in this way as much as he pleases, which will exercise the children's judgment, and also please them. But in order that the children may thoroughly understand what they are about, it is necessary to call a child, and cause him to count them himself, by placing them singly on the table. It must be observed, that it requires much patience, attention, and trouble, to give the children an insight into this part of the system; but the teacher will be amply recompensed for his pains. We have a number of little children who will readily answer almost any question in the multiplication, pence, addition, and subtraction tables. We have 100 of those cubes, and they may be placed in tens, fives, or in any way that the teacher

c

may think will be most advantageous to the scholar.

A method of giving little children bodily exercise, improving their minds, and pleasing them at the same time.

AS an infant school may be regarded be as a combination of the school and nursery, the art of pleasing forms a prominent part in the system; and as little children are very apt to be fretful, it becomes expedient to divert, as well as teach them; for if children of two years old and under are not diverted, they will naturally cry for the mother; and to have ten or twelve children crying in the school, would put every thing into confusion: but it is possible to have two hundred, or even three hundred children assembled together, the eldest not more than six years of age, and yet not to hear one of them crying for a whole day. Indeed I may appeal to the numerous and respectable personages, who have visited the school, for the truth of this assertion; many of whom have declared that they could not conceive it possible, that such a number of little children should be assembled together, and all be so happy as they have found them, many of them being so very young. But I can assure the reader, that many of the children who have cried heartily on being sent to school the first day or two, have cried as much on being kept at home, after they have been in the school but a very short time; and I am of opinion that when children are absent, it is frequently the fault of their parents. I have had children come to school without their breakfast, because it has not been ready; others have come to school without shoes, because they would not be kept at home while their shoes were mending; and I have had others come to school half dressed, whose parents have either been at work or gossiping, and when they returned home, have thought that their children had been lost; but to their great surprise and joy, when they have applied at the school, have found them there.

Can it be wondered at that little children should dislike to go to school, when in general forty or fifty, or perhaps more, are assembled together in one room, scarcely large enough for one third of that number, and who are not allowed to speak to, or scarcely look at, each other? In those places, I firmly believe, many, for the want of proper exercise, become cripples, or have their health much injured, by being kept sitting so many hours; but as the children's health is of the utmost consequence, it becomes necessary to remedy this evil by letting them have proper exercise, combined, as much as possible, with instruction; to accomplish which, many measures have been tried, but I have found the following to be the most successful, viz :—

The children are desired to sit on their seats, with their feet out strait, and to shut each hand, and then ordered to count an hundred, or as many as may be thought proper, lifting up each hand every time they count one, and bringing each hand down again on their knees when they count another. The children have given this the name of Blacksmith, and when they were asked why they called it Blacksmith, they answered because they hammered their knees with their fists the same way as the Blacksmiths hammered his irons with a hammer. When they have arrived at an hundred, (which they never fail to let you know by giving an extra shout,) then they may be ordered to sit on the ground, which they readily obey; they are then desired to take hold of their toes, which being done, they are desired to add up one hundred, two at a time, which they do by lifting up each foot alternately, all the children counting at one time, saying, two, four, six, eight, ten, twelve, and so on. By this means every part of the body is put in motion; and it likewise has this advantage, that by lifting up each foot every time, they keep good time, a thing very necessary, as unless this was this case, all would be confusion. They also add up three at a time by the same method, thus three, six, nine, twelve, fifteen, eighteen, and so on; but care must be taken not to keep them too long at one thing, or too long in one position.

Having done a lesson or two this way, they are desired to put their feet out straight, and their hands together, and to say, one and one are two, two and one are three, three and one are four, four and one are five, five and one are six, six and two are eight, and in this way they go on until they are desired to stop.

They also learn the pence and multiplication tables, by forming themselves in circles around a number of young trees that are planted in the play-ground; for the sake of order, each class has its own particular tree, and when they are ordered to the trees, every child knows which tree to go to; as soon as they are assembled around the trees, they join hands and walk round, every child saying the multiplication table until they have finished it; they then let go hands, and put them behind, and, for variety sake, sing the pence table, the alphabet, hymns, &c. &c: thus the children are gradually improved and delighted, for they call it play, and it is of little consequence what they call it, so long as they are edified, exercised, and made happy.

I have mentioned that the children say the multiplication table, &c. around the trees: this is calculated to impress it on their memory, and is adapted for fine weather, when the children can go out to play, as it is called. But in wet, or snowy weather, they cannot go out of the school, and it is then that we have recourse to the mode above mentioned; besides it is necessary that children should have exercise in winter, as well as in summer; in wet, as well as in dry weather; therefore there are several swings in the school-room, made of cord only, on which the children swing, two at a time. The time that they are allowed to be on the swing, is according to what they are going to repeat. If it is the pence-table, they say—

>Twenty pence are one and eightpence,
>　That we can't afford to lose;
>Thirty pence are two-and-sixpence,
>　That will buy a pair of shoes.
>Forty pence are three and fourpence,
>　That is paid for certain fees;
>Fifty pence are four and twopence,
>　That will buy five pounds of cheese.
>Sixty pence will make five shillings,
>　Which, we learn, is just a crown;

Seventy pence are five and tenpence,
  This is known throughout the town.
Eighty pence are six and eightpence,
  That sum once my father spent;
Ninety pence are seven and sixpence,
  That for a quarter's schooling went.
A hundred pence are eight and fourpence,
  Which is taught in every school;
Eight pence more make just nine shillings,
  So we end this pretty rule.

As soon as the table is thus gone through, the children who are on the swings get off, and others supply their places, until probably the pence table has been said twenty times; then we go on with the multiplication table, until the children have repeated as far as six times six are thirty-six; when the children on the swings get off, and are succeeded by two more on each swing; they then commence the other part of the table, beginning at six time seven are forty-two, until they have finished the table. At this time the children are all learning, not only those on the swings, but all those that are sitting in the school; and it is surprising to see with what alacrity the children will dispatch their other lessons, when they know it is a wet day, in order to get to the swings. Besides, they not only learn by this method, but it is admirably calculated to try their courage. Many little boys and girls, who at first were afraid to get on the swings, will swing now standing on one leg, and will, with the greatest dexterity, perform other feats, thus showing their courage in a great degree, and thereby causing them to be active. We generally let four or five children come to a swing, and those that can seat themselves first, are entitled to the first turn, for they are never lifted on. In their anxiety to get on the swing, some of them will perhaps get out of temper, especially those who are not disciplined; but those, on being detected, are not allowed to swing all that day, which soon makes them good natured to each other, and very cautious not to get into a passion. Thus, in some degree, their bad tempers are corrected, which is very desirable. As soon as two children are seated on each swing, to preserve order, the others retire (generally speaking) in the greatest good humor to their seats.

There is a swing for boys who are between five and six years old, another for those between four and five, another for the very little children, and another for the little girls; and on no account are children permitted to swing on the wrong swing, because if this was suffered, the strong would overcome the weak. But as the children opposed to each other, are mostly equal, those the most active, as I observed before, generally get the first turn, and not only this, it sets the children scheming. I have seen children about three years old try a number of plans, in order to get on the swing, that would have done credit to much older heads, and what perhaps may appear singular, we have had no serious accident since the introduction of the swings; and I am informed by Mr. Buchanan, who is master of the Westminster Infant School, that during the seven years he has been a teacher there, and at Mr. Owen's establishment, at New Lanark, that he never knew of any serious accident happening to any of the children.

Plan for teaching Infant Children by the aid of Pictures.

TO give the children general information, it has been found necessary to have recourse to pictures* of natural history, such as of birds, beasts, fishes, flowers, insects, &c. all

* See life of Dr. Doddridge:—"His parents brought him up in the early knowledge of religion before he could read, his mother taught him the history of the Old and New Testament, by the assistance of some Dutch tiles in the chimney of the room, where they usually sat; and accompanied her instructions with such wise and pious reflections, as made strong and lasting impressions upon his heart."

of which tend to show the glory of God; and as colours attract the attention of children as soon as any thing, they eagerly enquire what such a thing is, and this gives the teacher an opportunity of instructing them to great advantage; for when a child, of his own free will, eagerly desires to be informed, I think he will generally profit by such information.

There are also pictures of public buildings, and of the different trades; by the former, the children acquire much information, by explaining to them the use of the buildings, in what year they were built, &c; and by the latter, you may find out the bias of a child's inclination. Some would like to be shoe-makers, others builders, others weavers, brewers, &c.; in short it is both pleasing and edifying to hear the children give answers to the different questions. I have one little boy who would like to be a doctor; and when asked why he made choice of that profession, in preference to any other, his answer was, " because he should like to cure all the sick people." If parents did but study the inclinations of their children a little more than they do, I humbly conceive, that there would be more eminent men, in every profession, than there are. It is great imprudence to determine what business children may be adapted for, before their tempers and inclinations are well known; every one, says Horace, is best in his own profession—that which fits us best, is best; nor is any thing more fitting than that every one should consider his own genius and capacity, and act accordingly.

As it is possible that a person may be very clever in his business or profession, and yet not be a christian, it has been thought necessary to direct the children's attention to the Scriptures, even at this early age, and endeavour, if possible, to lay a solid foundation in the infant mind, and teach them to venerate the Bible, and to fear and love its Divine Author. The difficulties that laid in the way of attaining to so desirable an end, were many and various, the principal of which was, that they could not read well enough to peruse any part of the Bible. Some parents are quite delighted if their children can read a chapter or two in the Bible, and think that when they can do this, they have arrived at the summit of knowledge, without once considering, whether they understand one sentence of what they read; and how can it be expected that they should understand, when no previous groundwork has ever been attempted to be laid, at the time they receive their first impressions, and imbibe their first ideas? Every man comes into the world without a single innate idea, yet with a capacity to receive knowledge of every kind, and thereby capable of becoming intelligent and wise. In his infancy he would take hold of the most poisonous reptile, that would sting him to death in an instant; would attempt to stroke the lion with as little fear as he would the lamb; in short is incapable of distinguishing friend from foe. So wonderfully is man formed by his adorable Creator, that he is capable of increasing in knowledge, and advancing towards perfection to all eternity, without ever being able to arrive at it. The first thing that attracts his attention, even when in the cradle, is a light; and we may venture to say, the next things that attract his notice, are bright colours; it is for this reason, that pictures of Scripture history have been selected, such as Joseph and his brethren—Christ raising Lazarus from the dead—the Nativity—flight into Egypt—Christ disputing with the doctors—Christ baptized by John—curing the blind and lame—the last Supper—the Crucifixion—Resurrection—Ascension, &c. &c.

To begin with Joseph and his brethren, the following method is adopted:—the picture being suspended against the wall, and one class of the children standing opposite to it, the master repeats the following passages: " And Joseph dreamed a dream, and he told it to his brethren; and they hated him yet the more. And he said unto them, hear, I pray you, the dream which I have dreamed; for behold, we were binding sheaves in the field, and lo! my sheaf arose, and also stood upright; and, behold, your sheaves stood round about, and made obeisance to my sheaf."

The teacher being provided with a pointer, will point to the picture, and put the following questions, or such as he may think proper, to the children:—

Q. What is this?
A. Joseph's first dream.
Q. What is a dream?
A. When you dream, you see things in the time of sleep.
Q. Did any of you ever dream any thing?

Here the children will repeat what they have dreamed, perhaps something like the following. Please sir, once I dreamed I was in a garden.

Q. What did you see?
A. I saw flowers, and such nice apples.
Q. How do you know it was a dream?
A. Because, when I awoke, I found I was in bed.

During this recital the children will listen very attentively, for they are highly pleased to hear each other's relation. The master having satisfied himself that the children, in some measure, understand the nature of a dream, he may proceed as follows :—

Q. What did Joseph dream about first?
A. He dreamed that his brother's sheaves made obeisance to his sheaf.
Q. What is a sheaf?
A. A bundle of corn.
Q. What do you understand by making obeisance?
A. To bend your body, which we call making a bow.
Q. What is binding sheaves?
A. To tie them, which they do with a band of twisted straw.
Q. How many brothers had Joseph?
A. Eleven.
Q. What was Joseph's father's name?
A. Jacob, who is sometimes called Israel.

And it is further written concerning Joseph, that he dreamed yet another dream, and told it to his brethren, and said, behold, I have dreamed a dream more; and, behold, the sun and the moon, and the eleven stars, made obeisance to me.

Q. What do you understand by the sun?
A. The sun is that bright thing which shines in the day-time, and is placed in the sky.

Q. What is the sun composed of?
A. Fire, which gives heat and light.
Q. Who made the sun?
A. Almighty God.
Q. For what purpose did God make the sun?
A. To warm and nourish the earth, and every thing upon it.
Q. What do you mean by the earth?
A. The ground on which we walk, and on which the corn, trees, and flowers grow.
Q. What is it that makes them grow?
A. The heat and light of the sun.
Q. Does it reqnire any thing else to make them grow?
A. Yes, rain; and the assistance of Almighty God.
Q. What is the moon?
A. That thing which is placed in the sky, and shines in the night, and appears larger than the stars.
Q. What do you mean by the stars?
A. Those bright things that appear in the sky at night.
Q. What are they?
A. Some of them are worlds, and others are suns to give them light.
Q. Who placed them there?
A. Almighty God.
Q. Should we fear and love him for his goodness?

A. Yes, and for his mercy towards us.

Q. Do you think it wonderful that God should make all these things?

A. Yes.

Q. Are there any more things that appear wonderful to you?

A. Yes;—
Where'er we turn our wondering eyes,
  His power and skill we see;
Wonders on wonders grandly rise,
  And speak the Deity.

Q. Who is the Deity?
A. Almighty God.

In this way the teacher may go on, until be has placed before the children the leading facts in the history of Joseph, taking care, if possible, that the children understand every term used; and the teacher will find the children instructed and pleased, and himself none the worse for the exercise. He may also ask them the chapter, verse, name of the book, &c.

Lazarus raised from the Dead.

The picture being suspended as before described, we proceed thus:—

Q. What is this?
A. Jesus Christ raising Lazarus from the dead.

Q. Who was Lazarus?

A. A man that lived in a town, called Bethany, and a friend of Christ's.

Q. What is a town?

A. A place where there are a number of houses, and persons living in them.

Q. What do you mean by a friend?

A. A person that loves you, and does all the good he can for you, to whom you ought to do the same in return.

Q. Did Jesus love Lazarus?

A. Yes, and his sisters, Martha and Mary.

Q. Who was it that sent unto Jesus Christ, and told him that Lazarus was sick?

A. Martha and Mary.

Q. What did they say?

A. They said, Lord, behold, he whom thou lovest, is sick.

Q. What answer did Jesus make unto them?

A. He said, this sickness is not unto death, but for the glory of God.

Q. What did he mean by saying so?

A. He meant that Lazarus should be raised again by the power of God, and that the people that stood by, should see it, and believe on him.

Q. How many days did Jesus stop where he was, when he found Lazarus was sick?

A. Two days.

Q. When Jesus Christ wanted to leave the place, what did he say to his disciples?

A. He said, let us go into Judea again.

Q. What do you mean by Judea?

A. A city where the Jews lived.

Q. Did the disciples say any thing to Jesus Christ, when he expressed a wish to go into Judea again?

A. Yes, they said, Master, the Jews of late sought to stone thee, and goest thou thither again?

Q. What did Jesus Christ tell them?

A. He told them a great many things, and at last told them plainly that Lazarus was dead.

Q. How many days had Lazarus laid in the grave before he was raised up?

A. Four.

Q. Who went to meet Jesus Christ, when she heard that he was coming?

A. Martha; but Mary sat still in the house.

Q. Did Martha say any thing to Jesus, when she met him?

A. Yes, she said, Lord, if thou hadst been here, my brother had not died.

Q. Did Martha tell her sister that Jesus Christ was come?

A. Yes, she said, the Master is come, and calleth for thee.

Q. Did Mary go to meet Jesus Christ?

A. Yes; and when she saw him, she fell down at his feet, and said, Lord, if thou hadst been here, my brother had not died.

Q. Did Mary weep?

A. Yes; and the Jews that were with her.

Q. What is weeping?

A. To cry.

Q. Did Jesus weep?

A. Yes; and the Jews said, behold, how he loved him.

Q. Did the Jews say any thing else?

A. Yes, they said, could not this man that opened the eyes of the blind, have caused that even this man should not have died?

Q. What took place next?

A. He went to the grave and told the persons, that stood by, to take away the stone.

Q. And when they took away the stone, what did Jesus Christ do?

A. He cried, with a loud voice, Lazarus come forth; and he that was dead, came forth, bound hand and foot, with grave clothes, and his face was bound about with a napkin—Jesus saith unto them, loose him, and let him go; and many of the Jews which came to Mary, and had seen these things, which Jesus did, believed on him.

Q. If we wanted any more information about Lazarus and his sisters, where should we find it?

A. In the Bible.

Q. What part?

A. The eleventh and twelfth chapters of John.

I have had children at the early age of four years, ask me questions, that I could not possibly answer; and among other things, the children have said, when being examined at this picture, " that if Jesus Christ had cried softly, Lazarus, come forth, he would have came."—And when asked, why they thought so, they have answered, " Because God can do any thing;" which is a convincing proof, that children, at a very early age, have an idea of the Omnipotence of the Supreme Being.

Oh, that men would praise the Lord for his goodness to the children of men!

The Nativity of Jesus Christ.

The picture being suspended as the others, and a whole class being in the class-room, put the pointer in one of the children's hands, and desire the child to find out the Nativity of Jesus Christ. The other children will be on the tip-toe of expectation to see whether the child makes a mistake; for should this be the case, they know that one of them will have the same privilege of trying to find it; should the child happen to touch the wrong picture, the teacher will have at least a dozen applicants; saying, " Please, sir, may I; please, sir, may I." The teacher having selected the child to make the next trial, say one of the youngest of the applicants; the child walks round the room with the pointer, and puts it on the right picture; which will be always known by the other children calling out, " that is the right, that is the right." To view the child's sparkling eyes, who has found the picture, and to see the pleasure beaming forth in his countenance, you might imagine, that he conceived, he had performed one of the greatest wonders of the age. The children will then proceed to read what is printed on the picture, which is as follows: " The Nativity of our Lord and Saviour Jesus Christ;" which is printed at the top of the picture. At the bottom are the following words, " And she brought forth her first-born son, and wrapped him in swaddling clothes, and laid him in a manger, because there was no room for them in the inn."—We then question them in the following manner:—

Q. What do you mean by the Nativity of Jesus Christ?
A. The time he was born.
Q. Where was he born?
A. In Bethlehem of Judea.
Q. Where did they lay him?
A. In a manger.
Q. What is a manger?
A. A thing that horses feed out of?
Q. What was the reason they put him there?
A. Because there was no room in the inn.
Q. What is an inn?
A. A place where persons lodge who are travelling, and it is like a public house.
Q. What do you mean by travelling?
A. When we go from one place to another; from London into the country, or from the country into London.
Q. Is any thing else to be understood by travelling?
A. Yes; we are all travelling.
Q. What do you mean by being all travelling?
A. We are all going in a good road, or else in a bad one.
Q. What do you mean by a good road?
A. That which leads to heaven.
Q. What will lead us to heaven?
A. Praying to God, and endeavouring to

keep his commandments, and trying all we can to be good children.

Q. Can we make ourselves good?

A. No; we can receive nothing, except it be given us from heaven.

Q. What is travelling in a bad road?

A. Being naughty children, and not minding what is said to us; and when we say bad words, or steal any thing or take God's name in vain.

Q. Where will this road lead to?

A. To eternal misery.

Here we usually give a little advice according to circumstances, taking care always to avoid long speeches, that will tend to stupify the children. If they appear tired, we then stop, but if not, they repeat the following hymn, which I shall insert in full, as I believe there is nothing in it that any Christian would object to.

HARK! the skies with music sound!
Heav'nly glory beams around;
Christ is born! the angels sing,
Glory to the new-born King.

Peace is come, good-will appears,
Sinners, wipe away your tears;
God in human flesh to-day
Humbly in the manger lay.

Shepherds tending flocks by night,
Heard the song, and saw the light;
Took their reeds, and softest strains
Echo'd thro' the happy plains.

Mortals, hail the glorious King!
Richest incense cheerful bring;
Praise and love Emanuel's name,
And his boundless grace proclaim.

The hymn being concluded, we put the following questions to the children.

Q. Who was the new born king?
A. Jesus Christ.
Q. Who are sinners?
A. We, and all men.
Q. What are flocks?
A. A number of sheep.
Q. What are shepherds?
A. Those who take care of the sheep.
Q. What are plains?
A. Where the sheep feed.
Q. Who are mortals?
A. We are mortals.
Q. Who is the glorious king?
A. Jesus Christ.
Q. What is meant by Emanuel's name?
A. Jesus Christ.

Here the teacher can inform the children, that Jesus Christ is called by a variety of names in the bible, and can repeat them to the children if he thinks proper; for every correct idea respecting the Saviour which he can instil into their minds will serve as a basis or foundation for other ideas, and he will find that the more ideas the children have, the more ready they will be in answering his questions; for man is a progressive being; his progressions are his grand distinction; and those who would sink him to a level with the brute creation, must bring stronger arguments than they have hitherto done, before they will get the majority of mankind to believe them.

The flight into Egypt.

Q. What is this?

A. A picture of the flight into Egypt.

Q. What does flight mean?

A. To go from one place to another as quick as possible.

Q. Who went into Egypt?

A. Jesus Christ, with Joseph and Mary.

Q. What made them go into Egypt?

A. Because an angel told Joseph, in a dream, to go.

Q. What was the reason of their going?

A. For fear of Herod, a king.

Q. How long did they remain in Egypt?

A. Until an angel appeared to them again, and told them that Herod was dead.

These, and other questions, we put to the children, always taking care to watch their countenances, and the moment they appear tired we stop, and resume at another opportunity; for I find that one hour's instruction with the children's hearts, or wills, is better then twenty hours instruction when the children are thinking of something else.

To give an account of the whole of the Scripture Pictures would nearly fill a volume, and perhaps I have trespassed too much on the reader's time already; suffice it to say, that we have twenty-four of these pictures, all of which are used, besides twelve of Natural History, each picture having a variety of quadrupeds, birds, fishes, and flowers. The first thing we do is to teach the children the name of the different things, then to distinguish them by their forms, and lastly, they are questioned on them as follows;—if the animal is an horse, we put the pointer to it, and say,

Q. What is this?
A. An horse.
Q. What is the use of the horse?
A. To draw carts, coaches, stages, coal waggons, stage waggons, &c. &c.

Here we observe to the children, that as this animal is so useful to mankind, it should be treated with kindness; and having questioned them as to the difference between a cart and a coach, and satisfied ourselves that they understand the things that are mentioned, we close, by asking them what is the use of the horse after he is dead, to which the children reply, that its flesh is eaten by other animals; (naming them) and that its skin is put into pits, with oak bark, and is called tanning; and that when it is tanned it is called leather, and leather is made into shoes to keep the feet warm and dry, and that we are indebted to the animals for many things that we both eat and wear, and above all to the great God for every thing that we possess. I cannot help thinking that if this plan was more generally adopted, in all schools, we should not have so many persons ascribing every thing to blind chance, when all nature exhibits a God, who guides, protects, and continually preserves the whole.

We also examine the children concerning that ill-treated animal, the ass, and contrast it with the beautiful external appearance of the zebra, taking care to warn the children not to judge of things by their outward appearance, which the world in general is too apt to do, but to judge of things by their uses, and of men by their general character and conduct. After having examined the children concerning the animals that are most familiar to us, such as the sheep, the cow, the dog, and others of a similar kind, we proceed to foreign animals, such as the camel, the elephant, the tiger, the lion, &c. &c. In describing the use of the camel and the elephant, there is a fine field to open the understandings of the children, by stating, how useful the camel is in the deserts of Arabia; how much it can carry; how long it can go without water; and the reason it can go without water longer than most other animals; how much the elephant can carry; what use it makes of its trunk, &c. All these things will assist the thinking powers of children, and enlarge their understandings, if managed carefully. We also contrast the beautiful appearance of the tiger with its cruel and blood-thirsty disposition, and endeavour to show these men and women in embryo, that it is a dangerous plan to judge of things by appearances, but that there is a more correct way of judging, which forms a part of the business of education. But working people consider that education consists merely in the knowledge of letters and; perhaps, they are not the only persons who think so; at all events, few attempt to go beyond this with young children, for whom I am attempting to legislate. I may observe further, that all those persons who have visited the school, as far as I have been able to collect, have approved of the plan, and I do sincerely hope, that when the British public are made acquainted with the good that is doing, and is likely to be done, by this mode of teaching infants, that many will come forward and assist in establishing similar schools; not that I wish it to be understood that I hold up the school that I have charge of as a model for all others, no, when men of talent and penetration take up the subject, which I hope they will, we shall no doubt have much more light thrown upon it, which probably will be the means of establishing a system upon truly scientific principles. I have hitherto endeavoured to act as near nature as possible, without straining the thinking powers of children beyond their capacities: but should any better plan appear, I will most cheerfully (if permitted) adopt it. Some little fault has already been found with my mode of punishment, which I will notice in its proper place; in the mean time I requested those who differ from me, to suspend their judgment, until they hear what I have to say in defence. I have no other end in view, than the good of the children, who may be placed under my care, and I am satisfied, from the little experience I have had, that if the seeds of piety and virtue are sown early in the infant mind, they will not only prove a defence, but will mature and ripen, and finally triumph over vice and immorality. Let it also be distinctly understood, that I am not finding fault with those well regulated systems of instruction, known by the names of the Madras and Lancasterian systems; no, I am only pleading for children under the age of seven years; and I do hope, that the masters of those Institutions will find the children none the worse for being previously trained in an Infant School.—I would here appeal, in particular, to the ladies of England to exert their powerful influence in behalf of these infants, knowing that if they take it in hand it will prosper.

With these pictures, the children are highly delighted, and, of their own accord, require an explanation of the subjects. Nay, they will even ask questions that will puzzle the teacher to answer, and although there are in some minds such a natural barrenness, that, like the sands of Arabia, they are never to be cultivated or improved, yet I can safely say, that I never knew a child but what liked the pictures, and as soon as I have done explaining one, it is always, " Please sir, may we learn this? Please teacher, may we learn that?" In short, I find that I am generally tired before the children; for instead of having to apply any magisterial severity, they are petitioning to learn; and this mode of teaching possesses an advantage over every other, because it does not interfere with any religious opinion, there being no body of Christians that I know or ever heard of, who would object to the facts recorded in the Bible, being thus elucidated by pictures. Thus a ground work may be laid not only of natural history, but sacred history also; for the objects being before the children's eyes, they can, in some degree, comprehend them, and store them in their memories. Indeed there is such attraction in pictures, that you can scarcely pass a picture-shop in London, without seeing a number of grown persons around the windows, gazing at them. When pictures were first introduced into the school, the children told their parents, many of whom came and asked permission to see them, and although the plates are very common, I observed a degree of attention and reverence in the parents, scarcely to be expected, and especially from those who could not read.

By this plan, then, the reader will perceive, that the way may be paved, if I may be allowed the expression, almost to insure a desire in the children to read the Bible when they are able, and by their previous knowledge of the many leading facts contained therein, it is to be hoped that most of them will understand what they read, and consequently read day after day, with increased delight, until they have acquired such a love, veneration, and esteem for the sacred writings, that all the powers of evil will never be able to eradicate.

It is generally the case, that what we have always with us, becomes so familiar, that we set little store by it; but on being deprived of it for a time, we then set a greater value on it; and I have found this to be the case with the children and the pictures. If they were suffered to be exposed all at once, and at all times, then there would be such a multiplicity of objects before the children's eyes, that they would not fix their attention upon any of them; they would look at them all with wonder and surprize, and would cease to attract their notice, and, consequently, think no more of them than they would of the paper that covers the room. To prevent this, and cause the children to desire information, it is always necessary to keep some behind, and to let very few objects appear before them at one time, until they understand, in some measure, the subjects before them; afterwards they may be replaced by others, and so on successively, until they have seen the whole.

The human mind is susceptible of such an infinite variety, that it is continually seeking for new objects; and that which is the most beautiful, by being placed before our eyes too frequently, loses almost all its attraction, and ceases to claim our notice. Therefore, although the children are fond of this mode of teaching, unless it is managed with a proper degree of care, with an eye to please as well as edify, the children will be cloyed by having too much at once; and whatever good the teacher may wish to do for his little pupils, unless he particularly attends to this part of the subject, he will most certainly defeat his own objects.

I have spoken thus plainly, without the least design to offend any person who may now, or hereafter, have the charge of children; I only speak from what I have experienced, but others may have experienced differently; let them follow the plan that they think best; I have no wish to direct any one, for I find great need of direction myself; and if there is but one observation in this work that will tend to throw any additional light on the subject of the education of infant children, or that will be instrumental in improving the helpless and dangerous condition of the infant poor, and be the means of saving but one poor child, my end will be answered, and I shall be perfectly satisfied. I cannot dismiss this subject, without returning thanks to the Author of all good, that he should have strengthened the hearts of persons to venture even their lives, to improve the condition of the prisoners in Newgate, and elsewhere, and that females can be found, who will visit those abodes of vice and misery, to ameliorate the condition of their fellow creatures; this is a lasting honor to their sex, and I trust they will always retain their pre-eminence in endeavouring to do what is really good and useful. But it is acknowledged that prevention is better than cure; how much better is it then to endeavour to sow the seeds of virtue, piety, and holiness, in the infant mind, before it imbibes principles of dishonesty, and all the evils attending it! In the former, there are long confirmed habits, and preconceived opinion to contend against, but in the latter, there is more pliability of mind, and consequently more probability of success. It is well known, how hard it is to cultivate ground that has been over-run, for many years, with weeds of every sort, whereas if on their first appearance, they had been rooted up, then the good seed might have been sown to advantage, and, according to Scripture language, have produced fruit; some thirty, some sixty, and some an hundred fold.

The inclinations of children are frequently derived, hereditarily, from their parents, and as I have shown elsewhere, what is the conduct of many persons in the neighbourhood of the school, I trust it will be seen what good may be done, by taking the children out of the streets, before such inclinations are ripened; and thus nip them in the bud.

By those means many may be prevented from ever getting into a prison, and the number of those wretched and dangerous characters, it is to be hoped, will be considerably reduced. When once juvenile offenders find their way into those sinks of iniquity, there is very little hope of amendment. Indeed I conceive a prison has not the least terror to many; for it being a place of idleness, it calls forth the evil inclinations of its inmates, and as they have opportunities of indulging those evils, it loses all its terror. I heard a boy say, who had been confined in Newgate, that he did not care any thing about it; that his companions supplied him with plenty of victuals, and that there was some good fun to be seen there, and that most likely he should be soon there again; which proved too true, for he was soon after taken up again for stealing two pieces of printed calico, and transported. This will show that there are few who do not become more depraved, and leave that place worse than when they entered it.

On the Formation of Character.

IT is observed by a very celebrated writer, "that the educator's care, above all things, should be, first, to lay in his charge the foundation of religion and virtue." If then this is the first care, how important is it to take the first opportunity of instilling such principles into infant minds, before they are overcharged with principles of an opposite nature. It has likewise been observed, and perhaps, with some truth, "that the human soul is never idle, that if the mind is not occupied with something good, it must needs employ itself about something evil." The chief end and design of an infant school, is to keep the mind employed about what is innocent and useful; and therefore teaching children to read, write, and so on, are regarded as secondary objects. Many have been taught to read and write well, and have had, what is usually called, a good education; but inasmuch as they have not been taught their duty to God, and to each other, they have frequently launched out into every species of vice, and their education has only served to render them more formidable and dangerous to the rest of the community.

If we inquire the cause why men have been so loose in their principles, and vicious in their conduct, it seems to be, that in the places of education, of all ranks, until lately, too little attention has been paid to religious instruction. "Too many," says Dr. Fuller, "are more careful to bestow wit on their children, rather than virtue, the art of speaking well, rather than doing well;" whereas, their morals ought to be the chief concern: to be prudent, honest, good, and virtuous, are infinitely higher accomplishments, than being learned, rhetorical, metaphysical, or, that which the world usually calls, great scholars and fine gentlemen. A virtuous education for children, is to them a better inheritance, than a great estate: and here I cannot help observing, that much good might be done by establishing Infant Schools in Ireland; ignorance and idleness are the forerunners of much mischief, and it is well known that the lower classes of the Irish people have been much neglected in their education. At a meeting of the "Society for the promotion of Education in Scotland," at which one of the Royal Dukes presided, and who, likewise, took occasion to eulogize the Society, it was observed, that the effects of it were to be seen in the peaceable conduct of the poor in Scotland. Mr. H. in the course of the evening, said that about 100 years ago, the lower classes in Scotland were in the same ignorant and depraved condition as that in which the corresponding classes of Ireland were now. The only remedy for the evil in Ireland was in spreading education amongst them. He had been in three quarters of the globe, and he never was on a spot in which he did not find a Scotchman established; but the Scotchman was always found by him in a situation of trust.

We find, by sad experience, that children often imbibe vicious principles; while in their cradle they will watch our motions and notice our actions, and be those actions good or bad, they will copy them, and manifest them, in their own conduct, as soon as they are able. How extremely cautious, then, ought we to be, in whatever we do or say before children; and how zealous ought we to be in checking the very first appearance of evil in the infant mind. But how can this be done, without taking them out of the streets? will the parents do it? many cannot: the father goes to his daily labour in the morning, before the children are out of bed, and probably does not return until the children are in bed again at night. The mother, in many cases, goes out also, because the father's earnings will not support the family: in this case, if they were ever so disposed to instruct their children, they cannot do it; what then is the consequence?—

the children are intrusted to the care of some girl, whose parents, probably, are still poorer, and who are glad to let her earn something towards her support. I know numbers who go out in this way before they are twelve years old: those children are not qualified to check the first appearance of evil in their little charge: poor things! they have received no education themselves, but what they acquired in the streets, and this is readily taught those under their care, and it in general consists of deceit, lying, pilfering, and extreme filthiness. The parents are, perhaps, strangers to all these dangers to which their little ones are exposed; they inquire, when they come home, if the children have been good and quiet, and an answer in the affirmative is always ready. Let what will have happened during their absence, they will be kept in the dark concerning it, unless they are informed by some neighbour. I have known the children of such persons to be the pest of the whole neighbourhood. What kind of character can be expected from such tuition as this? Is it not a charity to take care of the children of such persons? most unquestionably it is.

There are other children, whose parents work at home, who are as bad off, if not worse; indeed, there are many children in the school, whose fathers are so lost to every principle of duty and humanity, that as soon as they receive their wages, they will go and get drunk, and leave their wives and children starving at home. When they return home, they will curse and swear, and beat both wife and children. I know many of this description, who care not whether their children curse and swear, lie and steal, as long as they can enjoy their pot-companions. One family in particular, I know, where there are seven children, two of which are in the school, and four of them are supported entirely by the exertions of the mother, who has declared to me, that she has not received one shilling from the father for a month together; all the money that he gets, he keeps to himself, and his family may starve and go naked for what he cares. He is not only a great drunkard, but a reprobate, and he beats and ill uses the poor woman besides. Again, I say, what can be expected from the offspring, with such an example as this before them? —the brutes are far before such men.*

---

* This man has since been called into the eternal world, where he must give an account of the deeds done in the body. His death was such as might be expected from such a character: he would have given a world for that consolation and serenity which is experienced by the man of piety and virtue. What a dreadful sight to see such a man in his dying

ON INFANT EDUCATION.

The dreadful effects of such examples are too prevalent in this, as well as other neighbourhoods; for some children even beat their parents. There is a poor widow, very near the school, who is frequently to be seen with her face dreadfully bruised by blows from her own son; he has been taken before a magistrate, and imprisoned for three months, but it has done him no good, for he beats his mother as much as ever, and the poor woman has it in contemplation to get the miscreant out of the country. One Sunday, I actually saw a boy, under twelve years of age, in the street, where the school is, take up a large stone to throw at his mother; the boy had done something wrong in the house, and the mother followed him into the street with a small cane, to correct him for it, but he told his mother, that if she dared to approach him, he would knock her down. The mother retired, and the boy went where he pleased. These, and many such scenes, I have frequently witnessed, and I am afraid, that many such characters have been so completely formed, as to be past reformation. So essential is it, in my humble opinion, to embrace the first opportunity of impressing on the infant

moments! and yet his family are more decent, and in every respect much better, than while he was here on earth.

mind, the principles of duty and virtue, that if this opportunity be lost, the worst consequences may follow.

The time for the children of the poor to receive instruction, and imbibe good principles, is between the ages of two and eight, for after that period, many are sent out to work, or detained at home, for they then become useful to their parents, and they cannot send them to school. There are many little girls who, after they have left the infant school, go out to work for one shilling a-week, and the mothers have declared to me, when I have endeavoured to persuade them to send their children to the National School for at least one year, that they could not do it, for they were so poor, that every shilling was a great help; they have promised me that they would send them to a Sunday school. This may account, in some measure, for there being so many more boys than girls, in almost every school in London, and shows the great good that has been done by Sunday schools.*

* It is to be observed here, that our children do not come to school on Sundays, but many of them between five and six years old, who have brothers or sisters in the National School, go with them to church, and others of the same age go to a Sunday school in the neighbourhood. In short, I may venture to say, that almost all the children that are able,

Several little girls who have been in the school, have formed such an attachment to it, that they come and ask leave to play in the school-room, after they have done work, with my own children, and it is no unusual thing to have twelve or fourteen little girls playing in the school-room or play-ground, in the summer evenings, until dark; sometimes we have as many little boys, but this is considered a very great favour, and on those evenings the girls do not come.

There are fruit-trees planted in the play-ground, to which the children will not do the least injury, nor will they touch the fruit. Flowers in pots, such as geraniums, auriculas, and other plants, are placed in the middle of the play-ground, without the least danger of being injured; thus they are taught to respect private property, and encouraged to inquire the names of the different plants and flowers, which I always tell them.

The children are permitted to bring their dinners with them, and there are boxes in the school to put them in. Every child in

---

go either to a Sunday school, or to church; but to take them all in a body, at the early age that they are admitted into our school, to any place of worship, and to keep them there for two or three hours, so as to profit them, and not disturb the congregation, is, according to my view, impracticable.

the school has access to these boxes, for they are never locked, and yet I have never known a child to lose his dinner, or any part thereof, notwithstanding many of the children, to my knowledge, have been kept extremely short of food. I have known an instance of a slice of bread and butter being left in the box for several weeks, by some child that could not eat it, but none of the other children would dare to touch it. I have found in the boxes two or three pieces of bread as hard as possible, and as a proof that many were hungry, and that it did not remain there because they could not eat it, but out of pure honesty, I have offered it to some of the children, and they have eaten it in that state. Cold potatoes, pieces of fat, &c. will not be unacceptable to them when given; but sooner than take any thing, without leave, they will actually let it spoil; these are facts that can be proved, and will show, that notwithstanding all the disadvantages to which poor children are exposed, their characters may be so far formed as to produce the effects above described. Would you take a piece of bread out of this box, that did not belong to you? said I to the children one day; no, Sir, replies a little girl of four years old—why not, because, says the child, it would be thieving. Well, but suppose no one saw you—Before I could speak another word, a number of the children answered—God can see every thing that we do—yes, added another little boy, if you steel a cherry, or a piece of pencil, it is wicked; to be sure, added another, it is wicked to steal any thing.

Questions of this sort have often elicited more than I ever expected; for children generally listen to conversation of this kind with pleasure, if it is not too long, and will often make observations and replies, that will prove beneficial to the teacher as well as to themselves, and tend greatly to promote the implantation of correct principles in their minds.

Here I will mention one circumstance which happened in the school, to show how necessary it is to teach by example as well as precept. Many of the children were in the habit of bringing marbles, tops, whistles, and other toys, to the school, which often caused much disturbance; for they would play with them instead of attending to their lessons, and I found it necessary to forbid the children from bringing any thing of the kind. And after giving notice two or three times in the school, I told them that if any of them brought such things they would be taken away from them. In consequence of this, several things fell into my hands, which I did not always think of returning, and among other things a whistle from a little boy. The child asked me for it as he was going home, but having several visitors at the time, I put the child off, telling him not to plague me, and he went home. I had forgot the circumstance altogether, but it appears the child did not, for some time after this, while I was lecturing the children upon the necessity of telling truth, and on the wickedness of stealing, the little fellow approached me, and said, "*Please, Sir, you stole my whistle.*" "Stole your whistle!" said I, "did I not give it you again?" "No, Teacher, I asked you for it, and you would not give it to me." I stood self-convicted, being accused in the middle of my lecture, before all the children, and really at a loss to know what excuse to make, for I had mislaid the whistle, and could not return it to the child: I immediately gave the child a halfpenny, and said all I could to persuade the children that it was not my intention to keep it. However I am satisfied that it has done more harm than I shall be able to repair for some time, for if we wish to teach children to be honest, we should never take anything from them without returning it again. Indeed persons having charge of children can never be too cautious, and should not, on any account whatever, break a promise; for experience has taught me that most children have good memories, and if you once promise a thing and do not perform it, they will pay very little attention to what you say afterwards. Children are such excellent imitators, that I have found they will not only imitate the conduct, but even the voice and expression of the countenance.

I have since learned that the little folks have a nick name for almost every thing. The scutcheons that they steal from off the keyholes, are called *porcupines*, brass weights, are called *lueys;* a loaf, a cheese, or any thing that they can lay their hands on, have all their respective names. When they have become proficients in these things, they are permitted to advance a step higher; for I have been told that they are not suffered to remain long at this work by their tutors, as their next step is to go into some chandler's shop, as sly as possible, and take an opportunity of stealing the till with its contents, there being always some older thief ready to take charge of it, as soon as the child brings it out of the shop; this is called *taking ding*. Many a poor woman has had to lament the loss of her till, with its contents, taken by a child, perhaps, scarcely six years of age. There is always a plan laid down for the child to act upon; should he be detected before he has actual possession of the till, he is instructed to pretend that he has missed his way, and inquires the way to some street near the spot; or, " please, ma'm," can you tell me what it is o'clock." The unsuspecting woman, perhaps, with the greatest kindness, shows the child the street he inquires for, and should she leave her shop for only one minute, she is sure to find herself robbed, when she returns, by some of the child's companions. Should he be detected in actual possession of the property, he is instructed to act his part in the most artful manner, by pretending that some man sent him into the shop to take it, who told him that he would give him sixpence to buy cakes. In short, it is impossible to get a knowledge of all the plans laid down by those delinquents for preying upon the public. Suffice it to say, that I have been in much personal danger, to obtain the facts that are here stated.

On the increase of Juvenile Delinquency.

IF any thing were wanting, to prove the utility, indeed I may say the necessity, of establishing Infant Schools in every part of the kingdom, in addition to what has been said, I might refer to the alarming increase of juvenile offenders, hundreds of whom carry on schemes that have the most direct tendency to make them, not only as they advance in years very dangerous members of society, but what are termed experienced thieves. Independent, then, of the good that may be done to them, as individuals, it becomes a public duty on our own account, to take the children of the poor out of the streets, and thus prevent them from falling into the hands of evil and designing persons, who make a living by encouraging the children of the necessitous poor to commit crimes, the produce of which they themselves take the greatest part.

The younger the children are, the better they suit the purpose of these vile miscreants; because, if such children are detected in any dishonest act, they know full well, that few persons would do more than give the child or children a tap on the head, and send them about their business. Thus the tenth part of the crimes, committed by juvenile offenders, never come under public view, because if any person should be robbed by a child, and should detect him, he is silenced by the by-standers, with this remark, "Oh! he is but a child, let him go this time, perhaps the poor thing has done it from necessity, being in want of bread." Thus the child is almost sure to escape, and instead of being punished, is not unfrequently rewarded for the adventure, as will be proved, from the following fact:—Having had occasion to walk through Shoreditch, not long ago, I saw a number of persons collected together around a little boy who, it appears, had stolen a brass weight from the shop of a grocer. The account that the shopman gave, was as follows: he stated, that three boys came into the shop for half-an-ounce of candid horehound, and that while he was getting down the glass which contained it, one of the boys contrived to purloin the weight in question. Having some suspicion of the boys, from the circumstance of having lost a vast number of brass weights, he kept his eyes upon them, and saw one of them put his hand into a box that was on the counter, and take the largest weight that was in it, and then run out of the shop, followed by the other two boys. The boy that stole it, slipt the weight into the hand of one of the others, and the shopman having observed this manœuvre, followed the boy that had the weight, who, being youngest of the three, could not run very fast, and finding himself closely pursued, threw away the weight into the road, and when he was taken, he declared that it was not him that took it. The man wished to take the child back to the shop, in order that his master might do with him as he thought proper, but the by-standers actually prevented him; and one man in particular seemed to interest himself much in the boy's behalf, stating that he knew the child very well, and that he had neither father nor mother. The child immediately answered that he had no father or mother, and that he had had no victuals all day: the individual before-mentioned then gave him one penny, and his example was followed by many more, and I think that the boy obtained nearly a shilling. I put several questions to the child, but was checked by this fellow, who told me, that as I had given the child nothing, I had no right to ask so many questions, and after giving me a great deal of abuse, ended by telling me, that if I did not take myself off, that he would give me something for myself. Feeling a great desire to sift still further into this mystery, I feigned to withdraw, but kept my eye upon the boy, and followed him for nearly two hours, until I actually saw him join the other two, one of whom I had not seen before, who had a bag with something very heavy in it, which I have every reason to believe contained weights, or something which they had obtained in a similar manner. Wishing to ascertain the fact, I approached the boys, who no sooner perceived me, than the little fellow who had been principal actor in the affair, called out, "*Nose, Nose,*" when they all ran down some obscure alleys. I followed, but was knocked down, as if by accident, by two ill-looking fellows, who kept apologizing to me, until the boys got out of the way. I cannot help thinking but that this was an organized system of depredation, and that the man, who took such an active part at the first, was at the bottom of all the business. I should be sorry to judge harshly of any person, but that individual's conduct was so mysterious throughout,—his activity in preventing the boy from being taken back to the shop,—his being the first to promote a subscription for the boy,—and, lastly, his threatening to give me something for myself, if I examined the child, all this I say, tends to confirm me in my opinion.

It is not unfrequent, however, that some of these youngsters are brought before the magistrates, as may be seen by the following case:—On the 17th of July, 1823, a child, only seven years old, was brought before the magistrates of Lambeth-street Office, charged with frequently robbing his mother, and in the end was ordered to be locked up all night in the gaol-room; but in the evening, when his mother returned, he forced his way out of the room, and behaved so violent, that they were obliged to iron both his hands and legs. It is evident to me, that this child had been in the hands of some evil disposed person, (probably unknown to the mother) who had given him a course of instruction, and without doubt, had begun with him very early. Who would suppose that it was necessary, in a country like this, to hand-cuff and fetter a child, at such a tender age; and how much training must he have previously undergone, to have become so exceedingly hardened, as to hold the magistrate, officers, and even his own parent, in defiance. This is another proof of the utility of Infant Schools. As the mind of a child expands, it searches for new objects or employment, to gratify that mind; this is the time that they fall an easy prey to those who make a business of entrapping them into the paths of dishonesty, and from that to crimes of a deeper die; and who is there amongst us, who would not rather prevent crimes than punish for the commission of them. I am happy under the consideration, that I was born in a country, where it seems to be the universal wish to prevent crime, and even after commission to punish as slightly as may be consistent with justice. One cannot view the exertions of the society for the improvement of prison discipline, without feelings of gratitude to those who take an active part in it. I will make a short extract from one of their reports, to shew that one of the acknowledged ends they have in view, is, the prevention of crime. They state, that " in the course of their visits to the gaols in the metropolis, the Committee very frequently meet with destitute boys, who, on their discharge from confinement, literally know not where to lay their heads. To assist such friendless outcasts has been the practice of the Society; and to render this relief more efficacious, a temporary refuge has been established for such as are disposed to abandon their vicious courses. This Asylum has been instrumental in affording assistance to a considerable number of distressed youths, who, but for this seasonable aid, must have resorted to criminal practices for support. On admission into this Establishment, the boys are instructed in moral and religious duty, subjected to habits of order and industry, and after a time are placed in situations which afford a reasonable prospect of their becoming honest and useful members of society.

To extend these objects, and to render its exertions more widely beneficial, the Society solicits the aid of public benevolence. Its expenses are unavoidably serious, and its funds are at present very low; but it is trusted that pecuniary support will not be withheld, when it is considered, that on the liberality with which this appeal is answered, depends in a great measure the success of the Society's objects—the reformation of the vicious, and the prevention of crime." I do think that if Infant Schools were to become general in this country, that a great deal of work would be taken off the Society's hands; and they would have the pleasure of seeing a number of children grow up, who had been fortunate enough to receive instruction and caution, through the instrumentality of an infant school, at an age when they most required it, who otherwise might have fallen into the Society's hands, and have ceased them a great deal of trouble. A gentleman, who visited the school, told me, that he had just left Newgate, and that he had been very much surprised at finding so many children there; some of whom were ironed; and on his inquiring the cause of so much severity with children so young, he was told by one of the turnkeys, that it might appear severe, but that he could assure the gentleman that he had much more trouble with them than he had with old offenders. This is by no means improbable, for the impressions that had been made upon those children, had formed, as it were, a part of their very lives, and being the first probably, were the strongest, and sooner than part with them, they would almost as soon part with life itself.

I have made it my business when the school has been over to walk round the neighbourhood, and make observations, to ascertain, if possible, what good has been done by the school; in these walks I have observed some things very pleasing, such as children playing at keeping a school, with a number of strange children, and observing the same rules and discipline as if they were really at school. I have also seen many children belonging to the school reproving others for saying bad words, or telling an untruth; and upon the whole I have perceived a very great amendment in the conduct and morals of the children, both towards their parents and playfellows. But I regret to say, that I have seen such scenes as human nature shudders at, and which I cannot here possibly describe. Indeed when I reflect on what I have seen, and upon the bad example which is set before infants, in low neighbourhoods, both by their own parents and almost all around them,—their open violation of every principle of truth; their blasphemous expressions in the ears of their children; their awful profanation of the Sabbath, and their total neglect of every thing holy and divine, I am truly astonished that crimes of every description are not more numerous. Let any person take a walk in the neighbourhood of Spitalfields, Bethnal Green, St. Giles's, St. Catherine's, Wapping, or in short, almost any poor neighbourhood, and he will be constrained to say that the situation of the infant poor is truly pitiable. It is my design to lay before the reader several lamentable instances of juvenile depravity, wherein will be shown the dreadful dangers that children are exposed to, and which will tend to solve a query put to me by a person who visited the school: viz. He wished to learn how it was that as there were so many experienced thieves detected every sessions, and sent out of the country, that we could not perceive any sensible diminution of crime, but others were always ready to supply their places? Doubtless many causes might be assigned why this is the case. It is my opinion that the principal cause is, that many such characters imbibe dishonest principles in their infancy both by example and precept, but had they been taken care of when young, I think that many of them might have become valuable members of society.

The first instance that I shall mention, is a crime that I am informed is very prevalent among children:—namely, three or four go together round the different squares, and with an old knife, or some such instrument, wrench off the brass work that goes over the key-hole of the area gates, &c. and sell it at the marine store shops; these boys are said to have sometimes received three or four shillings a day, by this means. Having a desire to be satisfied whether this was actually the case I have walked around many of the squares in town, and found that not one gate in ten had any brass-work over the key-hole, but I perceived that it had been wrenched off; a small piece of the brass still remaining on many of the gates. I am further informed, that when such children have become adepts in this art, the next step is to take the handles and brass knockers from doors, which is done by taking out the screw with a small screw-driver: these are disposed of in the same manner as the former; and they then progressively become qualified for stealing brass weights, &c. and very soon become expert thieves.*

* The following fact will show what extensive depredations, young children are capable of committing. I have inserted the whole, as it appeared in the public papers:—"*Union Hall; Shop Lifting.*—Yesterday, two little girls, sisters, very neatly dressed, one nine, and the other seven years of age, were put to the bar, charged by Mr. Cornell, linen draper, of High street, Newington, with having stolen a piece of printed calico, from the counter of his shop.

Mr. Cornell stated, the children came to his shop, yesterday morning, and whilst he was engaged with his customers at the further end of the shop, he happened to cast his eyes where the prisoners were, and

It is very dangerous for children to go out with coral necklaces, or with lace caps, for if unprotected they are likely to be robbed of them, and ill treated by boys scarcely ten years old; this is so common, that three children were robbed in one day, two in the

observed the eldest roll up a large piece of printed calico, and put it into her basket, which her little sister carried: the witness immediately advanced to her, and asked if she had taken any thing from off the counter; but she positively asserted that she had not. However, on searching her basket, the calico was found; together with a piece of muslin, which Mr. Cornell identified, as belonging to him, and to have been taken in the above way. Mr. Allen, questioned the eldest girl about the robbery, but she positively denied as to how, or in what manner the calico and muslin had got into her basket, frequently appealing to her little sister as to the truth of what she declared; when asked if she had ever been charged with any offence, "O yes sir, some time back, I was accused of stealing a watch from a house, but I did not do it." The magistrate observed, that the father should be made acquainted with the circumstances, and in the mean time, gave the gaoler instructions that the two little delinquents should be taken care of.

Hall, the officer, stated that he had information that there was a quantity of goods which had been stolen by the prisoners concealed in a certain desk in the house of the father; and that a great deal of stolen property would, in all probability be found there, if a search-warrant were granted, as the two unfortunate children were believed to be most extensive depredators.

Mr. Allen immediately granted the warrant; and Hall, accompanied by Mr. Cornell, proceeded to the residence of the father of the children, who is an auctioneer and appraiser, at 12, Lion-street, Newington.

Hackney Road, and one in the Kingsland Road, and a genteel little girl had her ear-rings taken from her ears by three boys, one of whom came behind her and put his hands over her mouth to prevent her crying out, while the other two took her ear-rings.

Hall returned in half an hour, with the father in his custody, and produced a great quantity of black silk handkerchiefs, which he had found on the premises, but the desk which had been spoken of by his informers as containing stolen property, he had found quite empty. The father, when questioned by the witness as to whether he had any duplicates of property in his possession, positively denied that fact. At the office he was searched and about fifty duplicates found in his pockets, most of which were for silk handkerchiefs and shawls. There were also a few rings, for the possession of which the prisoner could not satisfactorily account. He was asked why he had assured the officer he had no duplicates? He replied that he had not said so; but Mr. Cornell, who was present during the search, declared that the prisoner had most positively declared that he had not a pawnbroker's duplicate in his possession.

Mr. Watt, a Linen-draper, of Harper-street, Kent-road, stated, that he attended in consequence of seeing the police reports in the newspapers, describing the two children; he immediately recognized the two little girls as having frequently called at his shop for trifling articles, and added that he had been robbed of a variety of silk handkerchiefs and shawls, and he had no doubt but the prisoners were the thieves. It was their practice, he said, to go into a shop and call for a quarter of a yard of muslin, and while the shop-keeper was engaged, the eldest would very dexterously slip whatever article was nearest her to the little sister, who was

These are lamentable instances of juvenile depravity, and tend, among other things, to convince me that the principles of honesty, truth, and justice, cannot be sown too early in the human mind. Accordingly if any child in the school deprives another of any thing by force, however trifling the thing may be, even a pin, it is always noticed and never without a suitable admonition.

trained to the business, and thrust the stolen property into a basket, which she always carried for that purpose. Mr. Watt identified the silk handkerchiefs as his property, and said they had been stolen in the above manner by the prisoners.

The father was asked where he had got the handkerchiefs? He replied, that he had bought them from a pedlar for half-a-crown a piece, at his door. However, his eldest daughter contradicted him by acknowledging that her sister had stolen them from the shop of Mr. Watt. He became dreadfully agitated, and then said—"What could I say? Surely I was not to criminate my own children!"

Mr. Allen observed, that there was a clear case against the two children; but after consulting with the other Magistrates, he was of opinion that the youngest child should be given up into the charge of the parish officers of Newington, as she was too young to go into a prison; and desired that the other girl should be remanded, in order to have some of the pledged goods produced. The father was committed, in default of bail, for receiving stolen goods. The child has since been found guilty. The prosecutor stated, that the family consisted of five children, not one of whom could read or write.

A number of Facts and Anecdotes.

IT has been thought by many, that children are incapable of learning any thing useful, as it regards the ground-work of their future conduct in life, until they have attained the age of five or six years, but experience has proved that these opinions are by no means founded in truth; yet most of the public schools refuse to admit children until they are six or seven years of age. Not that I approve of children at the ages of five or six years, being in the same school with children who are ten, twelve, or fourteen, because I know by experience, that very great evils frequently follow from such an indiscriminate mixture, and that the elder children frequently push the little ones forward to mischief, and make them, as it were, a medium, to accomplish whatever end they may have in view, which they do not like to be seen in themselves, for fear of punishment. And not unfrequently do they teach them to say bad words, and put things into their heads that they would probably never have thought of; therefore I apprehend they do them more harm than good. I do not approve of such young children being sent to the same school with those so much older, for these and many more reasons; still I by no means approve of their being in the streets, for we are all well aware they can learn no good there. Indeed I have heard boys, hardly seven years old, make use of the most abominable expressions in their play. Any person who has been accustomed to walk the streets of London, must have heard many children take the name of the Almighty in vain, seldom or ever mentioning his most holy name, but to confirm some oath. I have seen boys playing at marbles, tops, and other games, who on a dispute arising about some frivolous thing, would call upon the Supreme Being to strike them deaf, dumb, or blind, nay even dead, if what they said was not true, when nevertheless I have been satisfied, from having seen the origin of their dispute, that the party using the above expressions has been telling a falsehood; indeed so common is this kind of language in the streets, that few persons notice it. I am inclined to think, that children being accustomed to say such words, on every trifling occasion, will, when they grow to riper years, pay very little respect to the sanctity of an oath. This, perhaps, is one of the reasons why we hear of so much perjury in the present day. At all events, little children cannot avoid hearing such expressions, not only from those who are rather older than themselves, but, I am sorry to say, even from their parents. I have had repeated instances of this kind. Many little children, when they first come to school, make use of dreadful expressions, and when I have told them it was wrong, some have said, they did not know it was any harm, and others, with the greatest simplicity, have told me, that they had heard their fathers or mothers say the same words. I have had much difficulty in persuading some children that it was wrong, for they very naturally thought, that if their parents made use of such expressions, that they might do the same. Hence the necessity of good example, and did parents generally consider how apt children are to copy them, both in their words and actions, they would be more cautious than they are. There are also many parents, who make use of very bad expressions themselves, that would correct their children for using the same; and as a proof of this, I will mention one circumstance, out of many others, that has taken place in this school. We have a little girl in the school, five years old, who is so fond of the school, that she frequently stops after school-hours to play with my children and some others, who chuse to stay in the play-ground, and many of them stop till eight or nine o'clock at night, to which I have no objection, providing their parents approve of it, and they do not get into mischief, as it is Mr. Wilson's wish to keep them out of the streets as much as possible. It happened that some of the children, one day, offended this child, and she called them dreadful names, such as I cannot mention here, but, of course, the other children were terrified at the expressions, and told me of them immediately. I was soon satisfied, that the child was ignorant of the meaning of what she said, and as an excuse for her conduct, she told me she heard her father and mother say the same words. I told the child, that notwithstanding her parents might have made use of such words, it was wrong, and very wicked, and that I could not let her stay another time to play, if she ever again made use of such words; and having sent for the mother, I told her the expressions the child made use of, but did not tell her what the child told me of her parents, for if I had, she would have beat the child most unmercifully. The mother, after having heard me relate the circumstance, immediately flew into a violent passion with the child, and declared, that she would skin her alive (this was her expression) and I had much difficulty to restrain her from correcting the child in the school. Having pacified her a little, I inquired where the child could have heard such wicked expressions. She said she could not tell. I then told her, I hoped the child did not learn them of her, or her father. To this, she made no answer, but I could perceive that she stood self-convicted, and having said what I conceived necessary upon the occasion, I dismissed her, observing, that it was useless for ladies and gentlemen to establish schools for the education of the infant poor, if the parents did not assist, by setting them a good example.

Here I am happy to observe, the advice I gave her, was not thrown away, as I have never known the child guilty of saying a bad word since; and the mother was very thankful, and soon brought me another child of two years and a half old, and said she should be very glad if I would take him in the school, and that she wished a blessing might always attend the gentlemen who supported the institution. She also requested me to take an opportunity of speaking a word or two to her husband, for she was thankful for what had been said to her. I mention this, to show that many parents, who are in the habit of using bad expressions themselves, do not always wish their children to do the same; in this way I conceive that good may not only be done to the children, but likewise to the parents themselves.

Our children are admitted as soon as they can walk, and we have several at eighteen months old, and from that age to six years.

There is a little boy now in the school,

whose name I shall omit mentioning, for reasons that will be obvious to the reader. Soon after he had been admitted into the school, his mother came to me with the following story, and as I made a memorandum of it at the time, I am enabled to give it in her own words:—" You see as how, Sir, this here little fellow, is only a little more than four years old, and you see as how, I and his father is obliged to go out at work all day, and I have four of them, and I can't leave nothing in the place for them, they break all my things, and this one thieves like any thing. He took a penny the other day out of a cup on the shelf at the top of the cupboard, and how do you think he done it? why, he put the table near the cupboard door, and on that table a chair, and then got on the top of both of them himself, and took the money. I put eighteen pence in the cup for my rent, and I just pop't home to give the children their dinners, when I saw my lord upon the table and chair, and I ax'd him what he was doing, and he said, nothing, mother, but I thought he was up to no good, so I looked at the rent, when, instead of finding eighteen pence, there was fourpence gone. I searched him, and found a penny in his pocket, and the others said as how he gave them some not to tell. Now, you see, Sir, this is a shocking thing, and I'd sooner see them all lie dead in the house, rather than see them come to a bad end, so I bought this here rod, and I mean to give him a good hiding before all the children, and I thinks as how, if any thing will shame him out of it, that will. I gives them all a belly full of victuals when we are both in work, and I'll be the death of them if they steal."

After this relation I kept a strict eye upon this child, and three or four days afterwards the children detected him opening my desk and taking halfpence out of it. The children informed me that he had been at the desk, and while they were bringing him up to me, the halfpence dropped out of his hand; I detected him in many other very bad actions, but have reason to hope, that by the aid of the *Green Tail,* and the *Old Broom,* he is effectually cured.

I recollect, a short time ago, seeing two little children, very near the school where I live, in close conversation, and from their frequently looking at a fruit-stall, that was near at hand, I felt inclined to watch them, having previously heard from some of the children in the school, that they had frequently seen children in the neighbourhood steal oysters, and different things. I accordingly placed myself in a convenient situation, and I had not long to wait, for the moment they saw there was no one passing, they went up to the stall, the eldest walking alongside the other, apparently to prevent his being seen, whilst the little one snatched an orange, and conveyed it under his pinafore, with all the dexterity of an experienced thief. Will it be believed that the youngest of these children was not four years old, and the eldest, apparently, not above five; and, from what I saw, I had good reason to believe it was not the first time these children had been guilty of stealing, though, perhaps, unknown to their parents, as I have subsequently found to be the case in other instances.

There is another little boy in the school, as fine a child as can be seen, whose mother keeps a little shop, but who could not prevail upon him to go to school, because some woman had threatened to put him into the black hole, therefore she was obliged to keep him at home. The mother stated to me that she could not always keep him in doors, therefore she wished to have him admitted into the infant school, as she had heard that the children were very happy and fond of the school, and observed, " perhaps my child may like to come to your school." The child was admitted and liked the school very well, but I was surprised to find that he frequently brought money to school, as much as threepence at a time. On questioning the child how he came by it, he always said that his mother gave it to him and I thought there was no reason to doubt the child's word, for there was something so prepossessing in his appearance, that, at that time, I could not doubt the truth of his story. But finding that the child spent a great deal of money in fruit, cakes, &c. and still had some remaining, I found it advisable to see the mother, and to my astonishment found it all a fiction, for she had not given him any, and we were both at a loss to conceive how he obtained it. The child told me, his mother gave it him, and he told his mother that it was given to him at school; but when he was confronted with us both, not a word would he say: it was evident, therefore, that he had got it by some unfair means, and we both determined to suspend our judgment, and to keep a strict eye on him in future. Nothing, however, transpsired for some time; I followed him home several times, but saw nothing amiss. At length I received notice from the mother, that she had detected him in taking money out of the till in her little shop. It then came out that there was some boy in the neighbourhood who acted as banker to him, and for every two-pence which he received from the child, he was allowed one penny for taking care of it. It seems that the child was afraid to bring any more money to school, on accouut of being so closely questioned as to where he got it, and this, probably, induced him to give more to the boy than he otherwise would have done. Suffice it, however, to say, that both children at length were found out, and the mother declared that the child conducted her to some old boards in the wash-house, and underneath them there was upwards of a shilling, which he had pilfered at various times.

I will add the following case of a little girl, under six years of age, who is now in the school, and whose mother is dead:— This child had been frequently absent from school, and was never at a loss for an excuse for such absence. As none of the children knew where she resided, I sent the eldest boy in the school with her, to ascertain whether her stories were always true, and gave positive instructions to them to make haste back; I saw no more of them for six hours, when the little boy returned, and told me that the girl would not show him where she lived; and that she had taken him so far, that, at length he was determined to leave her, but could not find his way back sooner. In the evening I went myself, according to the direction I had entered in the admission book, but found that the family were removed, and the persons in the house could not tell me where they were gone to reside. I saw nothing of the child for the five following days, when a woman who has the care of her and her little brother in arms, came to me to know the reason why the girl came home at such irregular hours, stating, that sometimes she came home at half-past eleven, at other times, not till two, and sometimes at three in the afternoon; in short, often an hour after school was over. I told her that the child was frequently absent, and that it was five days since I had seen her. The woman appeared quite surprised, and told me, that she had always sent the child to school at the regular time; that when she had come home before the usual time, she said her governess had sent all the children home a little sooner; and if she came home after the time, then she said that there had been some ladies visiting the school, and that the children had been kept for their inspection.

Here I must acknowledge, that I have frequently detained the children a little while after school hours, when we have had visitors, but since it furnishes the children with an excuse for going home late, I think it would be better to discontinue the practice; and have to beg of those ladies and gentlemen who may feel inclined to visit the school and see the children, that they will come between the hours of nine and twelve in the forenoon, or two and four in the afternoon. I have only to observe, that the child I have been speaking of, has come to school very regularly since, and I have no doubt but with care, she will become as fond of the school as any of the other children.

I could introduce a great number of facts of this description, but as they would be nearly similar, and tend to one and the same end, I shall forbear mentioning any more, except an anecdote or two, of a more pleasing nature; trusting, that as it has been shown that children are very early inclined to do that which is wrong, that, therefore, many persons, who heretofore thought differently, will now see that it is never too soon to endeavour to teach them what is right. When such young children commit a fault, it is generally passed over by their parents and others, with this observation, "O! he is but a child, and knows no better:" but it may be answered, perhaps, with some propriety, that they never will, unless they are taught; and I have shown, that thousands never have an opportunity of being taught, unless the pious and humane stretch forth

F

their hands, and snatch them from the many dangers by which they are surrounded.

I will insert part of a speech delivered by Mr. Sergeant Bosanquet, who presided for Mr. Justice Richardson, at the Gloucester Assizes, for April, 1823; of the truths of which I have daily proof: viz. "Gentlemen, I have reason to believe that the offences for trial on this occasion, are rather less than usual at this season, and, to whatever the diminution of crime may be ascribed, I cannot forbear earnestly to press upon your attention, a constant perseverance in two things, which, above all others, are calculated to diminish crime—the first, is an unremitted attention to the education of the children of the poor, and of all classes of society, in the principles of true morality and sound religion—the next is the constant and regular employment of such persons as may be sentenced to imprisonment in such labour as may be adapted to their respective ages and conditions.

"Gentlemen, I believe that these observations may be considered as quite superfluous in this county, and therefore I have taken the liberty of using the word perseverance, because I believe your attention is already strongly drawn to that subject, and it requires no exhortation of mine to induce your attention to it. I am not quite sure whether, in the gaol for this city, the same means are provided for the employment of those persons sentenced to terms of imprisonment, which are provided in the gaol for the county. Gentlemen, the magistrates for the city are equally desirous of promoting the education of all the poor under their care. I have no doubt, and I do hope and trust, if the means of labour have not been provided in their gaol, that no time will be lost in providing those means by which imprisonment may be made a real punishment, by which offenders may be reformed during their imprisonment, and by which the idle and dissolute may be prevented from any inclination to return there."

A little boy, the subject of the following anecdote, being six years of age, and forward in his learning, I considered him fit to be sent to another school, and sent word to the parents accordingly. The father came immediately, and said, he hoped I would keep him until he was seven years of age, adding, that he had many reasons for making the request. I told him, that the end and design of the Institution was to take such children as no other school would admit, and as his child had arrived at the age of six, he would be received into the National School; and as we had a number of applications to admit children much younger, I could not grant his request. He then said, "I understand that you make use of pictures in the school, and I have good reason to approve of them, for," said he, "you must know, that I have a large bible in the house, Matthew Henry's, which was left me by my deceased mother; but like many more, I never looked into it, but kept it merely for show. The child, of course, was forbidden to open it, for fear of it being spoiled; but still he was continually asking me to read in it, and I as continually denied him: indeed I had imbibed many unfavourable impressions concerning this book, and had no inclination to read it, and I was not very anxious that the child should. However, the child was not to be put off, although several times I gave him a box on the ear for worrying me; yet notwithstanding this, the child would frequently ask me to read it, when he thought I was in a good humour; and at last I complied with his wishes. 'Please, father,' said the child, 'will you read about Solomon's wise judgment,' I don't no where to find it, was the reply; 'then,' says the child, 'I will tell you; it is in the third chapter of the first Book of Kings.' I looked as the child directed, and found it, and read it to him. Having done so, I was about to shut up the book; which the child perceiving, says, 'now, please, father, will you read about Lazarus raised from the dead;' which was done; and in short," says the father, " he kept me at it for at least two hours that night, and compleatly tired me out, for there was no getting rid of him. The next night he renewed the application, with 'please, father, will you read about Joseph and his brethren', and he could always tell me where it was to be found. Indeed, he was not contented with my reading it, but would get me into many difficulties, by asking me to explain that which I knew nothing about; and if I said I could not tell him, he would tell me that I ought to go to church; for his master had told him, that that was the place to learn more about it, and added, ' and I will go with you, father.' In short, he told me every picture you had got in your school, and kept me so well at it, that I really got into the habit of reading for myself, with some degree of delight; this, therefore, is one of the reasons why I wish the child to remain in the school." A short time afterwards, the mother called on me, and told me, that none would be happier than she, for there was so much alteration in her husband for the better, that she could scarcely believe him to be the same man: that instead of being in the skittle-ground, in the evening, spending his money, and getting tipsy, he was reading at home to her and his children, and the money that used to go for gambling was now going to buy books, with which, in conjunction with the bible, they were greatly delighted, and afforded both him and them a great deal of pleasure and profit; that her object in calling, was once more to return thanks to Mr. Wilson, and myself for the great benefit that had accrued to the family, through the child being in the Infant School. Here we see that a whole family were made comfortable, and called to a sense of religion and duty, by the instrumentality of a child of six years of age; for I have made inquiries, and found that the whole family attend a place of worship, and that their character will bear the strictest investigation. By these means, the conditions of the working classes will be very much improved, and it seems to be the case already, according to the following extract from the Morning Chronicle:

"*Improvement of the Lower Orders.*--The statement of Sir Richard Birnie, on Monday, ' that he could not help remarking as a fact extremely creditable to the lower orders of people in this district, that the Magistrates never had so little to do in the way of night charges, as during the present holidays, even at ordinary seasons of the year,' has given us, in common, we trust, with all who take an interest in the improvement of the people, the greatest satisfaction. It would be doing great good, were Magistrates who have opportunities to make observations of this nature, to communicate them from time to time to the public. We have, ourselves, long been satisfied that a great change for the better has taken place in the habits of the labouring classes; and we are glad to have a confirmation of our opinion from such respectable authority. We attribute this reformation chiefly to the taste for reading, which has spread greatly of late years; for when a man acquires a taste for intellectual gratification, his relish for the beastly gratification of drunkenness, the cause of so many evils, is almost always diminished. A sort of revolution in the mode of selling books in this metropolis, and we believe the other large towns, has accompanied this fondness for reading. Formerly the copies of a book not disposed of within a given time, went to the trunk-maker; now the publisher, after a given time, has what is called a trade-sale, at which the undisposed-of copies are sold by auction; and in a day or two they are to be found exposed on all the stalls of the metropolis. When the bookseller has remunerated himself by a fair price from the more wealthy purchasers (which is generally the case), he can thus afford to let the labouring classes have the rest, at prices corresponding to their means. In this way excellent books often come into circulation among a class of people which used formerly to be strangers to all productions of the kind. The works of Smith, Paley, Hume, &c. are now in the possession of every mechanic. There is a general prejudice among ill-informed persons in easy circumstances, that the only way of keeping the lower orders sober and orderly, is to pay them the lowest rate of wages. The reverse is the fact, as is proved by the people of the metropolis, being more sober now, when the lowness of prices places so much more at their command, than they used to be when prices were high, and wages little different from what they are now. Whatever raises a man in his own estimation, and elevates his views, necessarily renders him more moral and sober. Hopeless, and ill-rewarded toil is the mother of all vice."

The following anecdote, will show how early impressions are made on the infant mind, and the effects such impressions have in the dying moments of a child. A little boy, between the age of five and six years, being extremely ill, prevailed on his mother to ask me to come and see him: the mother called, and stated, that he said he did want to see his master so bad, that he would give any thing if he could see him. The mother likewise said, she should be very much obliged to me if I would come; conceiving that the child would get better after he had seen me. I accordingly went, and on seeing the child, considered that he could not recover. The moment I entered the room, the child attempted to rise, but could not. "Well, my little man," said I, "did you want to see me." "Yes, sir, I wanted to see you very much," answered the child. "Tell me what you wanted me for." "I wanted to tell you that I cannot come to school again, because I shall die." "Don't say that," said the mother, "you will get better, and then you can go to school again." "No," answered the child, "I shall not get better, I am sure, and I wanted to ask master, to let my class sing a hymn over my body, when they put it in the pit-hole." The child having made me promise, that this should be done, observed, "you told me, master, when we used to say the picture, that the souls of children never die, and do you think I shall go to God?" "You ask me a difficult question, my little boy," said I; "Is it, sir," said the child; "I am not afraid to die, and I know I shall die." "Well, child, I should not be afraid to change states with you, for if such as you do not go to God, I do not know what will become of such as me; and from what I know of you, I firmly believe that you will, and all like you; but you know what I used to tell you at school:" "yes, sir, I do; you used to tell me, that I should pray to God to assist me to do to others, as I would that they should do to me, as the Hymn says; and mother knows, that I always said my prayers night and morning, and I used to pray for father and mother, master and governess, and every body else." "Yes, my little man, this is part of our duty, we should pray for every one, and I think, if God sees it needful, he will answer our prayers, especially, when they come from the heart." Here the child attempted to speak, but could not, but waved his hand, in token of gratitude for my calling, and I can truly say, that I never saw so much confidence, resignation, and true dependence on the divine will, manifested by any grown person on a death bed, much less by a child, under the tender age of seven years. I bid the child adieu, and was much impressed with what I had seen. The next day the mother called on me, and informed me, that the child had quitted his tenement of clay; and that just before his departure, had said to her, and those around him, that the souls of children never die; it was only the body that died; that he had been told at school, while they were saying the pictures, that the soul went to God, who gave it. The mother said, that these were the last words the child was known to utter. She then repeated the request, about the children singing a hymn over his grave, and named the hymn she wished to have sung.—The time arrived for the funeral, and the parents of the children, who were to sing the hymn, made them very neat and clean, and sent them to school. I sent them to the house, where the funeral was to go from, and the undertaker sent word, that he could not be bother'd with such little creatures, and that unless I attended myself, the children could not go. I told him, that I was confident, that the children would be no trouble to him, if he only told them to follow the mourners, two and two, and that it was unnecessary for any one to interfere with them further, than showing them the way back to the school. I thought, however, that I would attend to see how the children behaved, but did not let them see me, until the corpse had arrived at the ground. As soon as I had got to the ground, some of the children saw me, and exclaimed, "there's master;" and several of them stepped out of the ranks to favour me with a bow. When the corpse was put into the ground, the children were arranged round the grave, not one of whom were more than six years of age. One of them gave out the hymn, in the usual way, and then it was sung (according to the opinions of the by-standers) very well. The novelty of the thing caused a great number of persons to collect together; and yet, to their credit, while the children were singing, there was not a whisper to be heard; and when they were done, the poor people made a collection for the children, on the ground. The minister, himself, rewarded one or two of them, and they returned well stored, with money, cakes, &c. This simple thing was the means of making the school more known; for I could hear persons inquiring, "Where do these children come from?" "Why, don't you know," replies another, "from the Infant School, Quaker-street." "Well," answered a third, "I will try to get my children into it; for I should like them to be there of all things. When do they take them in, and how do they get them in." "Why, you must apply on Monday mornings," answered another, and the following Monday, I had no less than forty-nine applications, all of which

I was obliged to refuse, because the school was full. Should any persons, therefore, feel disposed to do good, and are possessed of the means, they can have an opportunity of doing so, by establishing another school in the vicinity of Spitalfields.

It is the practice with us, when a child arrives at the age of six, or at most seven years, to draft him to the National School, but should the parents disapprove of their children being sent there, they are at liberty to send them to what school they please.

Play Ground.

SINCE several schools have been lately established without this necessary appendage, I propose to say a few words on the subject. It appears to me, that without a play-ground, Infant Schools would be little superior to what are termed Dames' Schools, where the children of mechanics are usually sent; especially, as it regards the health of the children: indeed, in some instances, they would be worse, on account of the probability of their having more children than those Dames' Schools.

To have one hundred children, or upwards, in a room, however convenient such room might be in other respects, and not to allow the children proper relaxation and exercise, which they could not have without a play-ground, would materially injure their healths, which is a thing, in my humble opinion, of the first importance. I would rather see a school, where they charged two-pence or three-pence per week for each child, having a play-ground, than one where the children had free admission without one; for I think the former institution would do the most good. The play-ground may be compared to the world, where the little children are left to themselves, there it may be seen what effects their education has produced, for if any of the children are fond of fighting and quarrelling, it is there that they will do it, and this gives the master an opportunity of giving them seasonable advice, as to the impropriety of such conduct; whereas, if they were kept in school (which they must be, if there was no play-ground) then these evil inclinations, with many others, would never manifest themselves until they were in the street, and consequently, the master would have no opportunity of attempting a cure. I have seen many children, who would behave very orderly in the school, but the moment they get into the play-ground they manifest the principle of self-love to such a degree, that they would wish all the rest of the children to be subservient to them, and on some of the children refusing to let them bear rule, would begin to use force, in order to compel them to comply. This is conduct that ought to be checked, and what time can be so proper as the first stages of infancy?

I have had others, who would try every expedient, in order to deprive the weaker and smaller children of their little property, such as marbles, buttons, and the like; and when they have found that force would not do, they would try hypocrisy, and other evil arts, that are but too prevalent, and of which they see too many examples out of school. All these things have taken place in the play-ground, and yet in the school such children have shown no such disposition; consequently, had it not been for the play-ground, they would not have been detected, and those principles would have gone on ripening, until they had become quite familiar to the child, and ever after, perhaps, formed part of its conduct through life. I am so firmly convinced, from the experience I have had, of the utility of a play-ground, and for the above reasons, and many more that might be given, (were I not fearful that they would be too tedious to the reader) that I am the more anxious humbly to recommend that this necessary appendage to an infant school should not be dispensed with. I daily observe, that instead of playing in the streets, where there is scarcely any thing but evil before their eyes, the children will hasten to the school with their bread and butter in their hands, in less than a quarter of an hour after they have left it, knowing that they have an opportunity of playing there the remainder of their dinner time, so that they love the school, and but rarely wish to be any where else.

The play-ground of Mr. Wilson's school is paved with bricks, which I have found to answer very well, as they absorb the rain so quick, that ten minutes after a shower, the place is dry enough for the children to play in; which, perhaps, would not be the case with any other kind of paving. They are placed flat on the ground, but I should prefer them being put edgeways, as they would last many years longer, yet it would take nearly double the number of bricks by being so placed. If it is not paved, the ground will be soft, and the children will make themselves dirty. It should be so managed that the water may be carried off, for if there are any puddles, the children will get into them. Some persons have recommended a few cart loads of good iron-mould gravel, there being a sort that will bind almost like a rock, if well rolled, but the children are liable to dig holes if it is only gravel: if this is noticed in time it may be prevented; but if they are suffered to dig holes, and no notice is taken of it at first, it will be very difficult to prevent them from making a practice of it. If money can be saved, by any plan, perhaps it is as well to notice it; but after having weighed the advantages and disadvantages of gravelling, I am of opinion, that bricks are preferable. I should also recommend that fruit-trees be planted in the centre of the play-ground, and likewise round the walls; which will delight the children, and teach them to have respect to private property. There should also be a border of flowers round the play-ground, of such sorts as will yield the most fragrance, which will tend to counteract any disagreeable smell that may proceed from the children, and thereby be conducive to their health, as well as those who have charge of them. These things need be no expence to the establishment, except the purchase of them in the first instance, for they will afford an agreeable occupation for the master before and after school hours, and will prepare him in some measure for the duties of the day; and it will afford him an ample opportunity of instilling a variety of ideas into the minds of the children, and of tracing every thing up to the great First Cause. I have witnessed the good effects of these things, which makes me desirous of humbly recommending them to others. I prefer the objects of nature themselves, in preference to pictures, where they can be obtained; but the children should not, on any account, be allowed to pluck the fruit or flowers; every thing should be considered as sacred; for the end and design of these things is not only to give them ideas, but to prove their honesty. It must be a source of great grief to all lovers of children, to see what havoc is made by them in plantations near London, and, perhaps, grown persons are not entirely free from this fault; who are not content with a proper foot path, but must walk on a man's plantations, pull up that which can be of no use to them, and thereby injure the property of their neighbour. These things ought not to be, nor do I think they would be so common as they are, if they were noticed a little more in the training and education of children. It has been too much the practice with many, to consider the business of a school to consist merely in teaching children their letters; but I am of opinion, that the formation of character is of the greatest importance, not only to the children, but to society at large. How can we account for the strict honesty of the Laplanders, who can leave their property in the woods, and in their huts, without the least fear of it being stolen or injured; while we, with ten times the advantages, cannot consider our property safe with the aid of locks and bolts, brick walls, and even watchmen besides. There must be some cause for all this, and perhaps the principal one is, the defects in the education of children, and the total neglect of the infant poor, at a time when they should be taken especial care of; for conscience, if not lulled into sleep, but rather called into action, will prove stronger than either brick walls, bolts, or locks, and I am satisfied, that I could take the whole of my children into any gentleman's plantation, without their doing the least injury whatever.

On Rewards and Punishments.

AS man comes into the world, with a propensity to do that which is forbidden, it has been found necessary, at all times, to enact laws to govern him, and even to punish him, when he acts contrary to those laws; and where is the person, who will deny any man a just reward who has done any public act, whereby his fellow men have been benefited? Indeed it is an old, though homely maxim, "That the sweet of labour is the hope of reward." If, then, rewards and punishments are necessary to make men active, and to keep them in order, who are expected to know right from wrong, how can it be expected that children, who come into the world with hereditary propensities to evil, can be governed without some kind of punishment? I am aware, that I am not taking the popular side of the question, by becoming an advocate for punishment, but notwithstanding this, I must say, that I do not think any school in England has ever been governed without it, and I think that the many theories ushered into the world, on this subject, have not been exactly acted upon. Indeed it appears to me, that while men continue to be imperfect beings, it is not possible that either they, or their offspring, can be governed without some degree of punishment. I admit that punishment should be administered with prudence, and never employed but as a last resource. I am sorry to say, that it has descended to brutality in some schools, which, perhaps, is one reason why so many persons set their faces against it altogether. Although I have heard it asserted, that it is possible to manage one thousand children, entirely without punishment, yet I must confess, that I have never been able to find out a method to manage two hundred children without it.

But I shall lay before the public, fairly and candidly, the modes of punishment, that have been adopted in the Spitalfields Infant School, and leave them to form their own judgment.

The first thing that appears to me necessary, is to find out, if possible, the real disposition and temper of the child, in order to be able to manage him with good effect. I admit that it is possible to manage some children without corporeal punishment, and I have some in the school, at this present time, who, I believe, have never been punished, to whom a word will be quite sufficient, and who, if I were only to look displeased, would burst into tears. But I have others quite the reverse; you may talk to them till you are tired, and it would produce no more effect, half-an-hour afterwards, than if they were not spoken to at all. Indeed children's dispositions and tempers are as various as their faces; no two are alike; consequently what will do for one child, will not do for another; hence the impropriety of having any invariable stated mode of punishment. What should we think of a medical man, who would prescribe for every constitution alike? The first thing that he does, is to ascertain the constitution of the patient, and prescribe accordingly; and nothing is more necessary, likewise, for those who have charge of little children, than to ascertain their tempers and dispositions; having done this, as far as possible, should a child offend, they will, in some measure, know how to apply the necessary cure.

To begin with rewards; the monitors are allowed each, one penny a week: this was allowed by our benevolent founder, Mr. Wilson, at my own request, as I found much difficulty in procuring monitors; for whatever honors were attached to the office of a monitor, children of five years old could not exactly comprehend; they could much easier perceive the use of a penny; and as a proof how much they value the penny a week above all the honors that could be conferred upon them, I have always had a good supply of monitors, since the penny a week has been allowed. Before this, it always used to be, " Please sir, may I sit down, I do not like to be a monitor?" perhaps I might prevail on some to hold the office a little longer, by explaining to them, what an honorary office it was; but, after all, I found that the penny a-week spoke more powerfully than I did, and the children would say to each other, " I like to be a monitor now, for I had a penny last Saturday; and master says, we are to have a penny per week; don't you wish you was a monitor?" " Yes,

I do, and master says, if I am a good boy, I shall be a monitor by and by, and then I shall have a penny." I think they richly deserve the reward, for monitors are complete drudges; every monitor having to teach twenty, or more children, to spell one hundred words each, every morning, besides keeping them in order, and doing other things. This is not the only reward given as an encouragement to the children, Mr. Wilson having desired me, to give to some of the children, who attend regularly, a pair of shoes, whose parents cannot afford to purchase them. But in order to do good, it is necessary to be very cautious, and endeavour to ascertain if the parents can afford to pay for the shoes themselves; for I have found that some are mean enough to send their children with bad shoes, in order that they may have a pair given to them, when they themselves could well afford to pay for them. But there are others, to whom I have no doubt, the gift has been of real service, who have scarcely had bread to support their families, and consequently could not buy them shoes. In addition to the above rewards, many persons who have visited the school, have left a trifle to buy the children cakes, &c. so that on the whole, most of the children frequently get something.

With regard to punishments, they are

various, according to the disposition of the child. The only corporeal punishment that we inflict, is a pat on the hand, which is of very great service, for I have seen one child bite another's arm, until it has almost made its teeth meet; I should suppose few persons are prepared to say such a child should not be punished for it. I have seen others, when they first came to school, as soon as their mother has brought them to the door, begin to scream as if they were being punished, while the mother has continued threatening the child, and never putting one threat into execution. The origin of all this noise, has been because the child has demanded a halfpenny, as the condition of coming to school, and the mother, perhaps, has not had one to give him, but has actually been obliged to borrow one, in order to induce him to come in at the school door: thus the child has come off conqueror, and does just as he pleases with the mother. At this time I have made my appearance, to know what all the noise was about, when the mother has entered into a lamentable tale, telling me what trouble she has had with the child, and that he will not come to school without having a halfpenny each time he comes; but the moment the child has seen me, all has been as quiet as possible. I have desired the child to give me the halfpenny, which he has done directly, and I have returned it to the mother, and the child has gone into the school, as good as any child could do. I have had others, who would throw their victuals into the dirt, and then lie down in it themselves, and refuse to rise up, crying, " I will go home, I want to go into the fields, I will have a halfpenny." The mother answered, "Well, my dear, you shall have a halfpenny, if you will stay at school." " No, I want to go and play with Billy or Tommy;" and the mother at length has taken the churl home again, and thus fed his vanity, and nursed his pride, till he has completely mastered her to that degree, that she has been glad to apply to the school again, and beg that I would take him in hand.

I have found it necessary, under such circumstances, to enter into a kind of agreement with the mother, that she should not interfere in any respect whatever; that on such conditions, and such only, could the child be admitted; observing, that I should do by it the same as if it were my own, but that it must, and should be obedient to me; to which the mother has consented, and the child has been taken in again, and strange to say, in less than a fortnight, has been as good, and behaved as orderly as any child in the school. But I should deem myself guilty of duplicity and deceit, were I to say that such children, in all cases, could be managed without corporeal punishment, for it appears to me, that corporeal punishment, in moderation, has been the mode of correcting refractory children, from the earliest ages; for it is expressly stated in the Scriptures, "*He that spareth his rod hateth his son, but he that saveth him, chasteneth him betimes;*" and again, '*He that knoweth his Lord's will, and doeth it not, shall be beaten with many stripes.** There is certainly

---

* The following extract from the "Teacher's Magazine" will shew that corporeal punishment, in moderation, is not contrary to the Scriptures, and I hope will prove a sufficient defence for my *pat on the hand :—*

"The arguments of those whose opinions are *against* the question, appear to me to be both puerile and unsound, and directly at variance with the express declarations of Scripture. In matters where the Scriptures are silent, we are allowed to speculate, and to form our own opinions, according to the rules of propriety and common sense. But where the Scriptures exhibit positive injunctions to govern our conduct, we are not at liberty so to act.

Nothing can be plainer, than that the Sacred Oracles make corporeal correction an essential ingredient in the system of the religious training of the young. Prov xxii. 15, "Foolishness is bound up in the heart of a child, but the rod of correction shall drive it from him." Chap xix. 18, " Chasten thy son while there is hope, and let not thy soul spare for his crying." Chap xxiii. 13, 14, "Withhold not correction from the child, for if thou beatest him with the rod he shall not die. Thou

something very pleasing in the sound, that several hundred infant children may be well managed, kept in good order, and corrected of their bad habits, without punishment.

shall beat him with the rod, and shall deliver his soul from hell." Chap. xxix. 15—17, " The rod and reproof give wisdom, but a child left to himself bringeth his mother to shame. Correct thy son and he shall give thee rest; yea, he shall give delight unto thy soul." Chap. xiii. 24, " He that spareth his rod, hateth his son : but he that loveth him chasteneth him betimes." These declarations require no comment and if they *are* the words of inspiration, to argue and reason against their import must be impious. Moreover, both observation and experience testify, that where these injunctions are attended to, and judiciously mixed with pious instruction, the happiest effects are produced; while on the contrary, where these are neglected, and a system of indulgence and relaxation substituted, we see the most deplorable consequences ensue. And, indeed, what else can we expect, when man departs from the wisdom of God, and *leans to his own understanding*.

We know also that the Divine Administration proceeds according to the same method. It is an evident maxim of Scripture, that correction is the greatest proof of paternal love and regard, for " whom the Lord loveth he correcteth, even as a father the son in whom he delighteth." The wisdom of man says, the exercise of the rod or the cane excites evil passions in the breast of him who useth it, and alienates the affections of the children. But what says the Wisdom of God? " Correct thy son and he shall give thee rest: yea, he shall give delight unto thy soul." But, perhaps, it will be objected, that what is here insisted upon, belongs exclusively to parents, and will not apply to the

But as I have not been able to attain to that state of perfection, in the art of teaching, I shall lay before the reader, what modes of punishment have been adopted in the Spitalfields Infant School, and the success that has attended them.

The first offence deserving of punishment, which I shall notice, is playing the truant, and I trust I may be permitted to state, that notwithstanding the children are so very young, they do frequently, at first, stay away from the school, unknown to their parents; nor is this to be wondered at, when we consider how they have been permitted to range the streets, and get acquainted with other children of similar circumstances to themselves. When this is the case, they cannot be disciplined and brought into order in a moment; it is a work of time, and requires much patience and perseverance, to effectually accomplish it. It is well known, that when we accustom ourselves to particular company, and form acquaintances, it is no easy matter to give them up; and it is a

discipline of Sunday Schools: to which I would answer, that there is no other mode known or acknowledged in Scripture, for the religious training of children, but that given to parents, consequently, those who take upon themselves this charge, sit in the parents' seat, and are obligated to observe the same rules."

maxim, that a man is either better or worse, for the company he keeps; just so, it is with children, they form very early attachments, and frequently with children, whose parents will not send them to school, and care not where they are, so long as they keep out of their way. Then the consequence will be, that such children will persuade another to accompany them, and of course the child will be absent from school; but as night approaches, the child will begin to think of the consequences, and mention it to his companions, who will instruct him how to deceive both me and his parents, and perhaps, bring him through his trouble: this will give him fresh confidence, and finding himself successful, there will be little trouble in persuading him to accompany them a second time. I have had children absent from school, two or three half days in a week, and sometimes whole days, who have brought me such rational and plausible excuses, as completely to put me off my guard; but, who have been found out by their parents, from having staid out till seven, or even eight o'clock at night; the parents have applied at the school, to know why I kept the children so late, and have been informed that they had been absent all day. Thus, the whole plot has been developed, and it has been found that the children were sent to school at eight o'clock in the morning, and their dinners given them to eat at school; but instead of coming to school, they have got into company with their old companions, who, in many cases, I have found, are training for every species of vice. Some have been cured of truant playing, by corporeal punishment, when all other means I could devise, have failed. Others, by means the most simple, such as pinning a piece of green baize to their back, and making them walk round the school, when all the children, of their own accord, have called out, "*green tail, played the truant, green tail.*" This has had a most salutary effect upon some, as a means of prevention, as well as cure, who have actually caused their parents to come to me, and ask leave of absence for half a day, to rock a baby; and the parents have acknowledged, that they should not have come to ask leave, but the child had refused to stop at home, unless they did; alledging, that the child had told them, if he was absent without leave, he should have the *green tail.* Thus the parents have been brought into some degree of order through the instrumentality of their children.

When the *green tail* becomes too common, it loses its effect: it must then be laid by for a time, and something else substituted in its place, such as carrying the *old broom*, which is done in the following manner; the broom is placed on the offender's shoulder, and he or she has then to walk round the school, the children naming the crime, whatever it may be, and calling out *old brooms*; if it is for lying, they call out as follows; *told a lie, old brooms*. This punishment, will, in some degree, show the temper of the child: if he is passionate, before he has gone ten paces, he will throw the broom off his shoulder; but he must be made to take it up again, and walk as before, until he is conquered, when you may do almost any thing with him afterwards. But I have invariably found, that any child who has been subject to any of the above punishments, has never taken an active part, when another child has been similarly circumstanced, but in general, sits and holds down his head, as if sensible that it would ill become him to take an active part in the concern, knowing that he has been guilty of the same fault himself. This will make the child so conspicuous in the school, that all the children's eyes will be upon him for some time, and should he be absent, after he has been punished, the children themselves will find it out, and he is sure to be detected the first time; hence by keeping a strict eye upon him, he will begin to find new companions in the school, and form an attachment with some of his own school-fellows, and ultimately be as fond of his new companions, book, and school, as he was before, of his old companions and the streets. I need scarcely observe, how strong are our attachments, formed in early years at school; and I doubt not but many who read this, have found a valuable and real friend in a school-fellow, for whom they would do any thing within their power.

There are several children in the school, at this present time, who had contracted some very bad habits, entirely by their being accustomed to run the streets; and one boy in particular, only five years of age, was so frequently absent, and brought such reasonable excuses for his absence, that it was some time before I detected him. I thought it best to see his mother, and therefore sent the boy to tell her that I wished to see her: the boy soon returned, saying, his mother was not at home: the following morning he was absent again, and I sent another boy to know the reason, when the mother waited on me immediately, and assured me that she had sent the child to school. I then produced the slate, which I keep for that purpose, and informed her how many days, and half-days, her child had been absent for the last month; when she again assured me, that she had never kept the child at home a single half-day, nor had he ever told her, that I wanted to see her; at the same time observing, that he must have been decoyed away by some of the children in the neighbourhood; and regretting that she could not afford to send him to school before; adding, that the Infant School was a blessed institution, and an institution, she thought, much wanted in the neighbourhood. I need scarcely observe, that both the father and mother lost no time in searching for their child, and after a search of several hours, found him in Spitalfields market, in company with several other children, pretty well stored with apples, &c. which they had, no doubt, stolen from the fruit-baskets, that are continually placed there. They brought him to school, and informed me that they had given him a good flogging, which I found to be correct, from the marks that were on the child: and they stated, that they had no doubt but that would cure him. But, however, he was not so soon to be cured, for the very next day he was absent again, and after the parents had tried every expedient they could think of, without success, they delivered him over to me, telling me to do what I thought proper. Having tried every means that I could devise, with as little success, except the keeping him at school after school hours, though I had a great disinclination of converting the school into a prison, as my object was, if possible, to cause the children to love the school; and I thought I could not take a more effectual method of causing them to dislike it, than by keeping them, against their will, after school hours. But I at last tried this experiment, with as little success as the others, and was about sending the child out of the school altogether, as incorrigible. But I was unwilling that it should be said, that a child of only five years of age should master us. I therefore determined upon an expedient, which I have reason to think has had the desired effect; namely, we have a kind of guard in the school,* for the purpose of keeping the children from getting too near the stove, and it forms a kind of cage. In the summer this guard is put on an elevated situation, at one end of the school, and it struck me, that if I put him in there, it might do him some good. I accordingly procured a ladder, and placed him in it, taking care to prevent the possibility of an accident; he had scarcely been in five minutes, when the whole of the children, as if by common consent, called out, "Pretty Dicky, Sweet Dicky:" he immediately burst into tears, a thing very unusual with him, and I

---

* This has only been used once since, and now is entirely dispensed with.

must say, I was extremely glad to see it, and have to observe, that I have never known him absent without leave since, and what is more, he appears to be very fond of the school, and is now a very good child. Is not this, then, a brand plucked from the fire?

I have been advised to dismiss twenty such children rather than retain them by the above means, but if there is more joy in heaven over one sinner that repenteth, than over ninety and nine just persons who need no repentance, ought not such a feeling to be encouraged on earth? and likewise when it can be done by means, that are not injurious to the orderly, but on the contrary, productive of the best effects; for this child is now in the National School, with several others, who were as bad, or worse than himself, but, who scarcely ever fail to come and see me when they have a half holiday. Notwithstanding they have been subjected to the objected punishments, the master of the National School tells me, that neither of them have ever been absent without leave, and that he has no fault to find with either of them. I have further to observe, that the moment I perceive any bad effects produced by my method of punishment, that moment they shall be relinquished. I believe, that there is not a child in the school who would not be delighted to carry the broom, and even to have a piece of baize pinned to his back, if you would call it play; and the other children might laugh as long as they pleased, for he would laugh as hearty as any of them; and as soon as he had done, I should have a dozen applicants, with "Please sir, may I; please sir, may I;" but only change the name, and call it a *punishment*, and I should have no applications whatever, but they would dread it as much as they would a flogging. I am also aware, that this plan of punishment will appear childish and ridiculous; and, perhaps, it would be ridiculous to use it for older children, but with such young children I have found it answer well, and therefore have no wish to dispense with it; however, I shall take care not to encourage the children to ridicule each other while undergoing this or any other punishment, but (as I always have done) encourage them to sympathize and comfort a child as soon as his punishment is over; and I can truly say, that I do not recollect a single instance, when any children have been undergoing the broom or the baize punishment, but that some of the others would come and beg him off, with "please sir, may he sit down now;" and when asked the reason why they have wished to have the little delinquent forgiven, they have answered, "may be, sir, he will be a good boy." Well, their request has been complied with, and the culprit forgiven; and what have I seen follow? why, that which has taught me many an important lesson, and has convinced me, that children can operate on each other's mind, and be the means of producing, very often, better effects than adult persons can. I have seen them clasp the child round the neck, take him by the hand, lead him about the play-ground, comfort him in every possible way, wipe his eyes with their pinafore; ask him if he was not sorry for what he had done; the answer has been, "Yes;" and they have flew to me —" Master, he says, he is sorry for it, and that he will not steal again." In short they have done that which I could not do, and put me in possession of facts which, otherwise, I could never have known; and so won the child over by kindness, that it has caused the child not only to be fond of them, but equally as fond of his master and the school. To these things I attribute the reclaiming the children I have mentioned; and so far from it being productive of the "*worst effects,*" I have found it productive of the best.*

* The Master of the Bristol Infant Free School, in his address to the inhabitants of Bristol, thought proper to find fault with the mode of punishment adopted in the Spitalfields Infant School; but I should have thought that it would have been more prudent in him

The ill effects of expelling children as incorrigible, may be seen in the case of Hartley, who was lately executed, for he confessed before his execution that he had been concerned in several murders, and upwards of two hundred burglaries. We learn by the following account, that he was dismissed from school at nine years of age, and finding himself at full liberty, and there being no school-master who would be troubled with him, he immediately commenced robber. "Hartley's father formerly kept an inn (Sir John Falstaff,) at Hull, in Yorkshire. He was put to school in that neighbourhood, but his conduct at school was so marked with depravity, and so continually did he play the truant, that he was dismissed as unmanageable. He then, although only nine years of age, began with pilfering and robbing gardens and orchards, till at length his friends were obliged to send him to sea. He soon contrived to run away from the vessel in which he had been placed, and having regained the land, pursued his old habits, and got connected with many of the principal thieves in London, with whom he commenced

to have confined his observations to his own school, inasmuch as, very probably, his own mode of punishment would, upon examination, prove more objectionable.

business regularly as a housebreaker, which was almost always his line of robbery."

Should not every means have been resorted to, with this child, before proceeding to the dangerous mode of expulsion? for it is not the whole that needs a physician, but those that are sick; and I strongly suspect, that if punishment in the way of ridicule had been resorted to, it would have had the desired effect. I can only say, that there never has been a child expelled from tne Spitalfields Infant School, as incorrigible, nor do I think that there ever will. In conclusion, I have to observe, that the green baize and the broom punishment, is only for extraordinary occasions, and I think I am justified in having recourse to any means that are consistent with duty and humanity, rather than turn a child out into the wide world: but I will declare, that I will never have recourse to any means, for the punishment of a refractory child, that I would dislike to be used with one of my own, under similar circumstances.

On Cleanliness.

AS cleanliness is of considerable importance, not only to the children, but to those around them, it may not be amiss to take up a little of the reader's time upon this subject, and to state the different plans that have been devised, in order to make the children as clean as possible. For this end, Mr. Wilson caused a trough to be erected, and a pipe to convey the water into it, in order that the children might be kept clean; but before it had been up one month, it was ascertained, that instead of answering the end intended, it had quite a contrary effect, for the children would dabble in the trough, and actually make themselves ten times worse than they were, by wetting themselves from head to foot, which would frequently cause the children to take cold, of which the parents would complain. Some would take their children away, and take no notice about it; others would come and give the master, what they called, a "*good set down,*" and take their children away besides. It was, therefore, thought necessary to forbid the children washing themselves, and it was determined to wash all the children that came dirty. But it was soon found, that the dirty children increased so fast, that it required one person's time to attend to them; besides, it had another bad effect, as it encouraged the parents in laziness, and they would tell me, if I complained of their sending the children to school dirty, "That, indeed, they had no time to wash their children, there was a trough in the school for that purpose, and the persons who had charge of the school, were paid for it, and had a right to do it." In consequence of this, the trough was taken away, and it was represented to the parents, that it was their duty to keep their children clean, and that unless they did so, they would be sent home to be washed; and that if they persisted in sending their children without being washed, there would be no alternative left, but to dismiss the child from the school altogether. This offended some of the high-minded parents, and they took their children out of the school, but who, afterwards, petitioned to have them re-admitted. I mention this, merely to prevent others, who may be concerned in the establishment of an Infant School, from incurring an unnecessary expense, and to show that the parents will value the school, equally as well if you make them wash their children, as if you did it for them. The plan that we have acted upon, to enforce cleanliness, is as follows :—as soon as the children are assembled in the school, the monitors cause them to hold out their hands, with their heads up; they then inspect their hands and their faces, and all those who are dirty are desired to stand out, to be inspected by the master, who will easily perceive whether they have been washed that morning; if not, they are sent home to be washed, and if the mother has any decent pride in her, she will take care that it shall not often occur. But it may be found, that some have been washed, and have been playing with the dirt, when coming to school, which some children are very apt to do; in this case they have a pat on the hand, which generally cures them; but if this will not do, we put a little on the child's face, and make him walk round the school, the children all crying out *Sweep, Sweep, Sweep, Chimney Sweep*; I have never known this to fail. There is much trouble, at first, to keep the children quite clean; some of their parents are naturally dirty, and in such case the children will partake of the same quality; these children will require more trouble than others, but they will soon acquire cleanly habits, and, with proper management, will become as cleanly as any of the other children. As soon as a child is taken into the school, the monitor shows him a certain place, and explains to him, that when he wants to go into the yard, he is to ask him, and he will accompany him there. Of course there are separate accommodations for each sex, and such prudential arrangements made, as the case requires, and which it is unnecessary further to particularize.

Dimensions of a School-room capable of containing 300 Infant Children.

THE first thing which appears necessary to mention, is a plot of ground, and I should imagine that less than fifty feet wide, and one hundred feet deep, would not do; this will allow exactly fifty feet for a play-ground, deducting room for a building fifty feet square, and fourteen feet high, which ought to be the size of the school-room; but I am of opinion, that if the ground was one hundred and fifty, or two hundred feet deep, it would be much better, as this would allow one hundred or one hundred and fifty feet for a play-ground; which is of such importance, that I consider the system would be very defective without it; for it is there that the children manifest their true tempers and dispositions. There should likewise be a room, about fifteen feet square, to teach the children in classes, which may be formed at one end of the large room; and indeed this is absolutely necessary. The master and mistress should live on the premises: a small house, containing three or four rooms, would be quite sufficient for them. The reason for their living on the premises, is, because the children should be allowed to bring their dinners with them, as this will keep them out of the streets; besides, many of the children who go home to dinner will return in a very short time, and if there are no persons on the premises to take care of them, they will be lost; and not only so, but strange boys will come in from the streets, and do a great deal of mischief, if no one is there to prevent them.

The portion of sitting room that I have allowed for each child is twelve inches. The scholars should sit all round the school-room with their backs against the wall. A school-room of fifty feet square, deducting for the class-room and fire place, would hold one hundred and seventy children round the sides; to make room for the other one hundred and thirty, it would be necessary to have four forms to cross the school-room, two of them to hold thirty-two children each, and the other two, thirty-three each; but these forms should be put out of the way when the children go to play, otherwise they would fall over them and do themselves an injury. I would recommend that pulleys should be fixed to the roof, which would be very little expense, and cords passed through them; at the end of each form there might be fixed a staple, and at the end of each rope a hook, the hooks might then be put into the staples, and the forms drawn up, out of the way, by the master, in a minute or two; and when wanted, be let down in the same way; this would leave the whole space in the centre of the room vacant, a thing very desirable when the children are at play.*

The master's desk should be placed at the end of the school, where the class room is, by this means he will be able to see the faces of all the children, and they see him, which is extremely necessary, as they may then be governed by a motion of his hand.

On the ill consequences of frightening Children.

IT is common for many persons to threaten to put children into the black hole, or to call the sweep to take them away in his bag, when they do not behave as they ought; but the ill effects of this mode of proceeding may

* This has been objected to, it being thought dangerous to have forms suspended over the children's heads. If the forms are put out of the way, I care not by what method it is done; but I am convinced that with strong tackle they might be suspended as safe as the roof itself.

be perceived, by the following fact. There is a child in the school, who has been to one of those initiatory schools, where the children of mechanics are usually sent, called Dames' Schools, which was kept by an elderly woman, who, it seems, had put this child into the coal-hole, and told him, that unless he was a good boy, the black man would come and take him away; this so frightened the child, that he fell into a violent fit, and never afterwards could bear the sight of this woman. On the mother getting the child admitted into our school, she desired me to be very gentle with him, relating to me all the above story, except, that the child had been in a fit. About a fortnight after the child had been admitted, he came running one day into the school, exclaiming, "I'll be a good boy! master! master! I'll be a good boy." As soon as he caught sight of me, he clung round, and grasped me with such violence, that I really thought the child was mad; in a few minutes after this, he went off into strong convulsions, and looked such a dreadful spectacle, that I thought nothing less, than that the child would die in my arms. In this state he remained for about twenty minutes, and I expected that the child would be carried out of the school a corpse. I sent for the mother, and on her arrival, I perceived that she was less alarmed than myself, for she immediately said, that the child was in a fit, and that I had frightened him into it. I could only reply, by telling her, that she was mistaken, as the child had only just entered the school, and I was ignorant of the cause of his fright; but several of my little scholars soon set the matter at rest, by stating the particulars of the fright, as they saw it, when coming to school. It seems that there was a man passing along the street, who sweeps chimneys with a machine, and just as the little fellow passed him, he called out *sweep;* this so alarmed the child, that he thought the man was going to take him, and thus caused him to act as I have stated. The child, however, getting better, and the mother hearing what the children said, begged my pardon, for having accused me wrongfully, and then told me the whole particulars of his first fright with the woman, and the coalhole. I have the greatest difficulty imaginable, to persuade him, that a sweep is a human being, and that he loves little children as much as other persons. I believe that the child is not quite so terrified at the sight of a sweep, as he was, but he still talks something about old " Boge," and seems almost afraid to stir without company :* this shows

* This child is now in the School, and has had but one fit since.

how improper it is to confine children by themselves, or to threaten that they shall be taken away in a bag. Many persons continue nervous all their lives, through such treatment, and are so materially injured, that they are actually frightened at their own shadow.

It is also productive of much mischief, to talk of mysteries, ghosts, and hobgoblins, before children, which many persons are too apt to do. Some deal so much in the marvellous, that I really believe they frighten many children out of their senses. I can recollect, that when I was a youth, being frequently in the habit of hearing such stories, I have actually been afraid to look behind me. How many persons are frightened at such a little creature as a mouse, because the nature of that little creature has not been explained to them in their infancy. Indeed children should have all things shown them, if possible, that they are likely to meet with; and above all, it should be impressed upon their minds, that if they meet with no injury from the living, it is most certain, the dead will never hurt them, and that he, who fears God, need have no other fear.

On the Diseases of Children.

IT may, probably, be considered presumption in me, to treat on the diseases of children, as this more properly belongs to the faculty; but let it be observed, that my object is not to pretend to cure the diseases that children are subject to, but only to prevent those which are infectious from spreading. I have found that children between the ages of two and seven years, are subject to the measles, hooping-cough, fever, ophthalmia, and the small-pox; this last is very rare, owing to the great encouragement given to vaccination, and were it not for the obstinacy of many of the poor, I believe this disease would be totally extirpated. Since the opening of this school, I have only heard of three children dying of it, and those had never been vaccinated. I always make a point of inquiring, on the admission of a child, whether this operation has been performed, and if not, I strongly recommend that it should. If the parents speak the truth, I have but few children in the school who have not been vaccinated: this accounts, therefore, for having lost but three children through that disease.

The measles, however, I consider as a very dangerous disorder, and we have lost a great many children by this disease, besides two of my own. The symptoms I have generally found are as follow; it is preceded with a violent cough, and the child's eyes will appear watery; the child will also be sick. As soon as we perceive these symptoms, we immediately send the child home, and desire the parents to keep him at home for a few days, in order to ascertain if the child has the measles, and if so, the child must be prohibited from coming to school until well. This caution is absolutely necessary, as some parents are so careless, that they will send their children when the measles are thick out upon them.

The same may be said with respect to other diseases, for unless the persons who have charge of the school attend to these things, the parents will be glad to get their children out of the way, and will send them with various diseases upon them, without considering the ill effects that may be produced in the school. Whether such conduct in the parents proceeds from ignorance or not, I am not able to say, but this I know, that I have had many parents offer children, for admission, with all the diseases I have mentioned, and who manifested no disposition whatever to inform me of it. The number of children who may be sick, from time to time, may be averaged at from twenty to thirty-five. Out of two hundred and twenty, we have never had less than twenty absent on account of illness, and once or twice, we had as many as fifty.

Soon after we first took charge of the school, we found that there were five or six children in the school who had the measles; the consequence was, that it contaminated the whole school, and about eight children died, one of my own being of that number. This induced me to be very cautious in future, and I make a point of walking round the school twice every day, in order to inspect the children; and since the adoption of this plan, we have not had the measles in the school.

The hooping-cough is known, of course, by the child hooping; but I consider it the safest plan to send all children home that have any kind of cough; this will cause the mother to come and inquire the reason why the child is sent home; I then can ascertain from her whether the child has had the hooping-cough or not.

With respect to fever, I generally find the child appear chilly and cold, and who not unfrequently vomits. I do not, however, feel myself competent to describe the early symptoms of this disorder, but the best way to prevent its gaining ground in the school is to send all the children home who appear the least indisposed, and this will be the most likely way to prevent a fever from getting into the school. As to the ophthalmia, I can describe the symptoms of that disease, having had it myself, together with the whole of my family. It generally comes in the left eye first, and causes a sensation as if something was in the eye, which pricks and shoots, and causes great pain; the white of the eye will appear red, which is usually called bloodshot; this, if not speedily attended to, will cause blindness; I have had several children that have been blind with it for several days. In the morning the patients are unable to unclose their eyes, for they will be gummed up, and it will be some time after they are awake before they will be able to disengage the eye-lids. As soon as I observe these appearances, I immediately send the child home, for I have ascertained, beyond a doubt, that the disease is contagious, and if a child is suffered to remain with it in the school, the infection will speedily be spread among all the children.

As children are frequently apt to burn or scald themselves, I will here insert a method for the cure of both; it is very simple, and yet infallible; at least, I have never known it to fail. It is no other than common writing ink; one of my own children burnt its hand dreadfully, and it was cured by washing it all over with ink immediately. Several children have burnt their hands against the pipe, that is connected with the stove in the school-room, and have all been cured by the same means. One boy, in particular, laid hold of a hot cinder that fell from the fire, and it quite singed his hand; I applied ink to it, and it was cured in a very short time. Let any one, therefore, who may happen to receive a burn, apply ink to it immediately, and he will soon witness the good effects of the application. This is mentioned with no other end than to do good; the author has found it cure himself and numbers around him, and therefore is desirous that it should be generally known.

Plan to prevent Accidents at School.

AS children are very apt to get into danger, even when at school, it becomes expedient to exercise the utmost vigilance, in order to prevent the possibility of an accident; for where two hundred children are assembled together, and all at play, the eldest not exceeding seven years of age, it is most certain, that if there be any danger, some will get into it.

All the doors on the premises should be so secured, that the children cannot swing them backwards and forwards, for if they are not, some of the children will get their fingers pinched. The forms also, should be so placed, that the children may not be likely to fall over them. Every thing should be put out of the way, that will be likely to occasion any danger to thoughtless children.

On the dangers Children are exposed to between the ages of two and seven years.

I SHALL begin this section by noticing some of the most prominent dangers to which the children of the poor are liable, and hope to be able to convince the unprejudiced mind, that it would be a charity to take charge of the infant poor, and thus preserve them from falling into danger; even leaving the idea of their learning any thing good at school entirely out of the question. There are some persons who seem to have a very great aversion to the poor being instructed at all; and I confess that I have been in company, where I have been more surprized than edified at the conversation on this head; some contending that since the establishment of so many schools in the country, they could not keep a servant, and that many servants idled away their time, in reading novels, instead of attending to their business, and that upon the whole it has made their servants so high-minded, that they can scarcely be spoken to, and in consequence they have condemned the system of educating the lower orders, on this very account. But it appears to me that a man might just as well condemn eating and drinking, because there are persons to be found who abuse the former by making gluttons of themselves, and the latter by getting intoxicated. Besides the principle in itself is such a selfish one, that it surprizes me how any person should encourage it for a moment: that because a person is poor, he should be deprived of all the means of obtaining knowledge. If, indeed, talent were confined to those in a high sphere of life, there might be some reason for advocating the cause of ignorance: but it must be admitted, that many persons of the meanest extraction, and in different countries, have become men of considerable eminence, by having an opportunity given them, for the development of their talents and abilities, which otherwise would have been lost to themselves and their country, many of whom have left names behind them that will never be forgotten. But it still remains to be proved that ignorant servants are the best, and until that is done, I trust there will always be found persons, who will advocate the cause of the uneducated poor.

I am not without hopes, that even those persons, who disapprove of educating the poor at all, will see the propriety of keeping, if possible, the children of the poor out of danger, and thus contribute to save the lives of many little ones, who would otherwise be lost to their country, by the many accidents that are likely to occur.

I have mentioned before, that the poor are unable to take that care of their children which their tender age requires, on account of their occupations, and have shown that it is almost certain, that the children of such persons will learn every species of vice. But there are other kind of dangers which more immediately affect the body, and are the cause of more accidents than people in general are aware of.

It is well known that poor people are frequently obliged to live in garrets, three or four stories high, with a family of six or seven children; and it frequently happens that when the children are left by themselves, two or three of them will come tumbling down stairs, some break their backs, others their legs or arms; and to this cause alone, perhaps, may be traced a vast number of cripples that daily appear in our streets.

When the poor parents return from their daily labour, they sometimes have the mortification of finding that one, or probably two, of their children, are gone to an hospital; this of course makes them unhappy, and unfits them to go through their daily labour. This dead weight, which is continually on the minds of the parents, is frequently the cause of their being unable to please their employers, and in consequence they are frequently thrown out of work altogether; whereas if the parents were certain that their children were taken care of, it is most likely that they would proceed to their daily labour cheerfully, and be enabled to give more satisfaction to their employers than they otherwise could do.

It is much to be regretted that those persons who most need employ, should be the last to procure it, for there are so many obstacles thrown in the way of married persons, and especially those with a family, that many are tempted to deny that they have any children for fear they should lose their situation.

Indeed it appears to me that it is an additional stimulus to a servant to behave orderly, when he knows that he has a family to look to him for support; and it is a proverb, often quoted by the poor, "*That God never-sends children without the means of supporting them,*" and I verily believe this to be the fact.

I prefer the more noble method that has been taken by that eminent philanthropist, Mr. Owen, who, instead of throwing obstacles in the way of HIS PEOPLE, does all he can to make them happy; he not only finds employment for the parents, but actually finds persons to take care of their children, for which purpose suitable buildings have been erected, and all other conveniences supplied for educating, and thus training them to become useful members of society.

He has erected a building capable of containing the children of the whole of *his people*, and of course suitable persons to take charge of them. And, as far as I know, Mr. Owen is the first person with whom originated the idea of educating infant children, upon an extensive scale.* I am not aware, however,

---

* It appears from an extract of Mr. Brougham's speech in the House of Commons, that the first Infant School established in England, was by himself and friends at Brewer's Green, Westminster, but since that period the plan has been considerably improved.

"Mr. Brougham was of opinion the house should be cautious of sanctioning the plan submitted to them, as it might end in disappointment, and indispose the people to such as were really practicable. For himself, he thought the opinions of Mr. Owen unfounded, and differed from many of them altogether. In the details of the plan however there was much deserving of notice, particularly what related to the training of children He thought a Committee ought to be appointed to inquire into that most important branch of the subject.

that Mr. Owen published any separate system on the management of infant children, for what he said on the subject is so interwoven with the other part of his plan, that it would not be very easy for any one to select a number of rules, so as to be able to form a system capable of being generally adopted for children in any other part of the world.

It must also be recollected that as all the people at New Lanark are employed by Mr. Owen, the parents, as a matter of course, would prefer sending their children to his establishment for various reasons; and therefore whatever plans this gentleman may propose, he can adopt them, without in the least endangering the stability of his school; because his school is not so liable to fluctuate

The children were only taken from their parents in the day time, who by that means were enabled to work for their maintenance, and the good habits acquired by the children, had a good effect on the morals of their parents. An experiment on that subject, in which several benevolent individuals had concurred with himself, was then trying not far from that place. Mr. Owen was a most candid and liberal projector; and on the occasion to which he had alluded had given one of his own superintendants. The school to which he had before adverted, was on Brewer's Green, Westminster, which was open at all times to those who wished to inquire into the nature of the plan that he and his friends had adopted. He should vote for a Committe to inquire into what parts of the plan might appear to be practicable, and to separate those from the rest."—*Vide Statesman, Dec.* 17, 1819.

as others, and the parents being in some degree of order themselves, will be more likely to accede to any thing which he may have to propose. But it is not so in London, for there it is quite the reverse; the parents are employed by different persons, in different places, and in consequence assume an air of independence; therefore, unless the mode of teaching meets their approbation, they will not send their children at all to school; and I think I may venture to say, that there is not one tenth part of the difficulties to contend with at Lanark, that we have to encounter in London, nor are the children exposed to so many dangers. I do not mean to insinuate that the people at New Lanark are not independent, as far as persons in their sphere can be, but what I mean to say is, that the local advantages and circumstances are so very different, that what might answer very well at Lanark, would require some alteration to be adapted for London, and to be accomodated to the inhabitants therein.

I have known parents who, being obliged to go out, have locked their children in a room to prevent them from getting into the street, or falling down stairs, and who have taken, as they imagined, every precaution to protect their children; but the little creatures, perhaps, after fretting and crying for hours at being thus confined, have ventured to get up to the window, in order to see what was passing in the streets and to gratify their little minds, when one, overreaching itself, has fallen into the street and been killed on the spot. There are cases enough of this kind daily to be met with in the public papers, and hundreds of accidents have occured, that are not noticed in the papers at all.

I have mentioned in a former part of this work, that many children are burnt to death, or run over for want of proper care. It is likewise astonishing, what numbers are lost by strolling into the fields, and falling into some pond, are drowned. In short, they are surrounded by so many dangers, that it becomes a public concern, and speaks to the hearts of all the pious and humane, and calls loudly upon them to unite their efforts to rescue this hitherto neglected part of the rising generation from the imminent dangers to which they are exposed.

Having taken the liberty of mentioning the name of Mr. Owen, I take this opportunity of returning my sincere thanks to that gentleman, for having visited the Spitalfields Infant School three or four times. He has been pleased to express his approbation of the system there pursued, and during these visits has dropped many useful hints, for which I beg most humbly to thank him; and here I may observe, that I could not have brought the school to its present state, had I not received some assistance. Mr. Wilson has likewise rendered that assistance which he saw necessary, and which has been productive of much good. He also pays me my salary, and all other incidental expenses that may in any way be thought necessary in furtherance of his benevolent design; he likewise visits the school frequently, though with much inconvenience to himself, to inspect the school and give me advice. Suffice it to say, that by the exertions of this gentleman, the neighbourhood has been very much improved, and the school so much respected among the poor, that we have at this time no less than 223 children, the whole of whom have come unsolicited on our part, the parents applying of their own free will to have their children admitted. Were the premises sufficiently capacious for containing 300 children, I have not the least doubt but we should soon have that number; and what is more, the general appearance of the little ones is so much improved, that there is no comparison to be made between them now, and what they were, when the school first opened.

Let any one picture to himself what would be the state of the infant poor if there were one or two such schools in every parish—the parents would be made perfectly happy, knowing that their children were secure from all harm, and the children themselves would be happy in being associated with children of the same age, exchanging ideas with each other to the mutual advantage of the whole;—evil of every description banished from their view—their time passing away in innocent and useful recreation, and every opportunity taken for instilling into their infant minds the principles of truth, piety, and virtue, and all that can form the Christian; at an age too when, like thirsty ground, ever ready to imbibe the dew and rain, they are so anxious for information, and ready to receive all you have to offer for their acceptance.

Had such then been generally the case, how many would have become useful servants of the common-weath who, through being neglected in their infancy, have spent half their time in prison, and have caused a great expense at last to send them out of the country. My pen would fail, were I to attempt describing the hundredth part of the good that might be done, were such schools to become general: by this means, evil would be attacked before it had gained a strong hold, and the number of offenders, instead of increasing, it is to be presumed, would materially diminish. Besides, the children, by being accustomed to order at such an early age, would be far more pliant and easier instructed when they were removed to another school, and in consequence, half the drudgery would be taken off the teacher's hands.

As I have had much experience from being brought up in London, I am perfectly aware of the snares and dangers that the children of the poor are liable to fall into; and therefore most solemnly affirm, that nothing, in my view would do so much good to the community at large, as the taking care of the infant children of the poor.

With regard to the expense, I have ascertained beyond a doubt, that according to the plan adopted in Mr. Wilson's school, 300 children may be taken care of, from the age of eighteen months to seven years, and instructed in every thing that such children are capable of learning, for £150. per annum,* which is ten shillings a year for each

---

* It is to be observed, that I am speaking of a free-school. In Mr. Wilson's school the children pay nothing; but some persons have wished that the children should pay a penny or two-pence per week; this of course would considerably diminish the expenditure, and I have no doubt that in country villages, and in decent neighbourhoods, it might be obtained. But in such neighbourhoods as Spitalfields, St. Catherines, some parts of St. Giles's, Wapping, &c. &c., many of the parents are not able to pay, and many that are, would sooner let their children run the streets than pay a penny: yet the children of the latter persons are the greatest objects of charity.

child. This includes the salary for the master and mistress; the salary for a third person to do the drudgery; coals, slates, cards, and every other thing requisite for the school, except the rent of the premises; I question whether it does not cost the country as much for every two individuals that are transported out of it. I am informed, that in some of the States of America, there is a law to compel parents to send their children to school, and that schools are accordingly provided by the government, and that this is considered as no hardship by the inhabitants, but rather as a blessing.* This law, however, does not take effect until the children are eight years of age; how far such a law would be advisable in this country, I will not pretend to say; but if crimes in the two countries be compared together, it will be found that it is five to one against us. Two were cast for death, the last sessions under twelve years of age; and Miles, who was executed, was very

* I was informed by the same gentleman, who is an inhabitant of one of the States, that this plan answers so well, and the people so generally approve of it, that the schools have become very rich, by persons leaving them property, and that they had more money than they knew what to do with in that channel; it is to be hoped that when our Trans-Atlantic friends hear of infant schools being approved of in this country, they will soon find another channel for the overplus money.

young: but if all were to be executed who had sentence of death passed upon them, there would be from fifteen to thirty executed every sessions in London, Middlesex, and Surrey. This, I think, would be more than are executed in Scotland and America put together; and what is most remarkable, in Scotland and America, education is more universally diffused and encouraged than in any other place on earth. I have thought that it might be practicable to establish one or two infant schools in every parish in England, by imposing a tax of one shilling a year upon every family, and every servant in place, (both male and female,) the family, I should think would have no objection to pay such a trifling sum, if they had the privilege of sending their children to school for it; and the latter I should conceive would pay it cheerfully, knowing that they themselves had derived many advantages from similar institutions; the rich would not have any objection surely to pay so trifling a sum, although they would receive no immediate benefit from the plan, otherwise than perhaps being saved the expense of prosecuting certain individuals who, probably, had it not been for the good impressions that had been made upon them in an infant school, and further matured in a National, British, or a Sunday school, might have committed some crime, so as to have rendered the former proceeding necessary; and I should imagine, that there is not a person, possessing the least spark of humanity, who would not rather pay a tax that would tend to prevent a child from falling into danger, than to be compelled to pay a tax for the express purpose of punishing him after he had fell into it. Perhaps no tax could be imposed but what would be considered unjust by some persons, and yet they would have no objection to reap the benefit arising from it. The only objection I could see to such a plan, would be on the score of religious opinions, for if any attempt was to be made to insist upon the children being taught any particular religious sentiments, or that the schools should be under the superintendence of any individuals of particular religious sentiments, to the exclusion of all others, such an attempt no doubt would be extremely unpopular, and I for one should object to the plan; but if these things were to be done upon truly liberal principles, and an opportunity given to both Churchmen and Dissenters to have schools, and schoolmasters, according to their own choice, without any interference on the part of the legislature, as to these particulars; I do think that such a tax, with the generality of well-disposed persons, would be far from being objectionable. With respect to the collection of this tax, that would be an after consideration; but no doubt care would be taken to have no useless drones in the concern; and further, that in its collection, the public should be put to the least expense possible. If the poor, generally speaking, could see the propriety, as well as the necessity of keeping their children out of the streets, where there is nothing but bad example before their eyes, and of sending them to school at the earliest age, there would be no necessity for a tax, for they would cheerfully come forward and voluntarily throw in their mite; but this is not the case, many of them do not see the danger, until it comes upon them, therefor eit behoves those who are the guardians of us all, and who are gifted with much clearer perceptions, to endeavour to avert the danger; and where the poor will not do that which would evidently be for their own good, as well as that of their children, I can see no impropriety in compelling them to do it, providing the religious scruples of many, before mentioned, are not lost sight of; for we have certainly no right to compel a man to have his child taught that which he deems to be error. No doubt there are many leading truths which might be taught children, that few persons would object to, and these might be taught generally; but where certain points have been subject to controversy, without coming to any final decision, such points might be avoided as a law of compulsion, and left to the majority of those to decide, who are most interested therein. I have merely thrown out these thoughts, without wishing them to be acted upon, unless they appear reasonable and proper. I merely give my opinion, the value of which must be estimated by my readers; I can only say, that I would most willingly pay my share of the tax, come when it would; but if never adopted, I shall not feel grieved, so long as the public could see the necessity of taking care of children, and forming schools or asylums for their protection. The means by which such a desirable object could be accomplished, would be of little consideration to me; but I thought if I could give any idea that would tend to facilitate it, I was in duty bound so to do.

I will mention a practice that is very prevalent among the poor, and which does more mischief than people are generally aware of, and that is, sending their children to the pawnbrokers. It is well known that many persons send children, scarcely seven years of age, to these places, with pledges of various sorts, a thing that cannot be too severely condemned. I know an instance of a little boy finding a shawl in the street, who being in the habit of going to the pawnbroker's for his mother, he, instead of taking the shawl home to his parents, actually pawned it, and spent all the money, which might never have been known by his parents, had not the mother found the duplicate in his pocket. It is evident then, that many parents have no one but themselves to blame, for the misconduct of their children, for had this child not been accustomed to go to such a place for his parents, he would never have thought of going there for himself; and the shawl most likely would have been carried home to his parents, which he ought to have done. Indeed there is no knowing, where such a system will end, for if children are suffered to go to such places, they may in time pledge that which does not belong to them; and this is such an easy way of turning any article into money, that we find most young thieves, of both sexes, when apprehended, have a few duplicates about them. Those persons, therefore, who take pledges of children (contrary to the Act of Parliament) whether they know it or not, ought to be severely reprimanded; for I am persuaded, that such conduct is productive of very great mischief indeed.

There is another thing also which is productive of much harm, and that is, taking children to fairs. The first year our school was opened, when there was any fair near London, there used to be seventy or eighty children absent; but the parents have been almost cured of this, for at this present time we have not had above twenty absentees to go to a fair, and several of the children have told me, that their parents wished to take them to the fair, but they requested to be permitted to go to school instead. Indeed the parents, finding that they can enjoy themselves better without their children, now generally leave them at school.

It is a difficult matter to persuade grown persons of the impropriety of attending fairs, who have been accustomed to it when children; but children are easily persuaded from it; for if they are properly entertained at school, they will not have the least desire to attend fairs.

I shall conclude this section by relating one or two more very bad habits that children are addicted to, which are, perhaps, fit subjects for the *Mendicity Society;* for as it is the object of that society to clear the streets of beggars, it would be well if they would put a stop to those juvenile beggars, many of whom are children of respectable parents, who assemble together to build what they call a GROTTO; and, to the great annoyance of all passengers in the streets, by begging for money. However desirous persons may be of encouraging ingenuity in children, I think it is doing much harm to give them money, in the streets, when they ask for it. Indeed it appears that some of the children have learned the art of begging so well, that they are able to vie with the most experienced beggars. I have witnessed many ladies very much annoyed by children getting before them and asking for money, who would not take an answer when given them, but put their hats up to the ladies' faces, and say, " please ma'am, remember the grotto," and when they were told by the parties that they had no money to give, would still continue to follow, and be as importunate as any common beggar. However innocent and trifling this may appear to some, I am inclined to believe that such practices tend to evil, for they teach children to be mean, and may cause some of them to chuse begging rather than work: I think that the best way to stop this species of begging, is never to give them any thing. I shall relate a fact which came under my own observation, as a proof that the system is productive of mischief. A foreign gentleman was walking up Old-street-road, and when he came to the corner of one of the streets, he was surrounded by three or four boys, saying, "Please, sir, remember the grotto."—" Go away, I will give you none." "Do, pray sir, remember the grotto." " No, I tell you I will give you nothing."—" Do sir, only once a-year." At length, I believe, he put something into one of their hats, and thus got rid of them, but he had scarcely gone two hundred yards, before he came to another grotto, and out sallied three more boys, with the same importunate request: he replied, "I will give you nothing; the devil have you and your grotto." The boys still persevered, till the gentleman, having lost all patience, gave one of them a gentle tap, to get out of the way, but the boy being on the side of the foot path fell into the mud, which had been scraped off the road, and in this pickle followed the gentleman, bellowing out, "That man knocked me down in the mud, and I had done nothing to him." In consequence, a number of persons soon collected, who insulted the gentleman very much, and he would certainly have been roughly handled, had he not given the boy something as a recompence; he increased his enemies, by calling all the English a set of beggars, and after bestowing various other epithets upon our country, which I cannot name, called a coach, declaring he could not walk the streets in safety.

Those who know what mischief has arisen from very trifling causes, will, of course, perceive the necessity of checking this growing evil; for this man went away with very unfavourable impressions concerning our country, and would, no doubt, prejudice his countrymen against us, and make them suppose we are worse than we are. Nearly allied to this, is "Pray remember poor Guy Faux;" which not only teaches children the art of begging, but is frequently the means of their becoming dishonest, for I have known children break down fences, and water-spouts, and, in short, any thing that they could lay their hands upon, in order to make a bonfire, to the great danger of the inhabitants near it, without producing one good effect; yet how easy might this practice be put down. The ill effects of it are so self-evident, that there can be no need for enlarging upon it. I also disapprove of children going about begging at christmas, which practice is calculated to instil into the children's minds a principle of meanness not becoming the English character, and the money they get, seldom or ever does them any good. If persons choose to give children any thing at this time of the year, I think there can be no solid objection to it, but l cannot bear to see children going about to ask for money like common beggars; it cannot be proper, and should be generally discountenanced. These things, with many others, may appear trifling, but to me they are of some consequence; for if we mean to improve the general character of the labouring population, there is nothing like beginning in time; and we should then soon get rid of those mean, improper, and barbarous customs.

Qualifications of a Master and Mistress.

PERHAPS no one has felt his own insufficiency, in any situation, more strongly than I have, since I took charge of the Spitalfields Infant School, which induces me to make a few observations on the qualifications of a master and mistress. It is a very common idea, that almost any person can educate little children, and that it requires little or no ability; but it will be found, however, that this is a great mistake, for if it be the business of such a person to lay the foundation of religion and virtue in the infant mind, with every grace that can adorn the christian character, there must be something more done than merely saying a few printed lessons by rotation, without knowing whether the children really understand what they say. How frequently may we find children, ten or twelve years of age, who cannot answer the most simple question, and who nevertheless have been to school for years. Giving the children ideas, is a part of education seldom thought of; but if we really wish to form the character, and improve the condition of society generally, there must be some attention paid to these things; and I should think that little need be said to prove, that few ideas are given in dames' schools. There may be a few of these schools, where an exception may be made; but generally speaking, where the children of mechanics are usually sent, before the age of seven years, no such thing is thought of. The mind of a child is compared, by Mr. Lock, to a sheet of blank paper, and if it is the business of a tutor to inscribe lessons on this mind, and to make it productive, it will require much patience, gentleness, perseverance, self-possession, energy, knowledge of human nature, and above all, piety, to accomplish so great a work.

Whoever, therefore, is in possession of these requisites, may be considered as a fit and proper person to manage an infant school, and whoever has charge of such an institution will find plenty of opportunities to display each of these qualifications. It would be almost useless to attempt to cure the bad tempers of children, if the master should encourage and manifest such evil tempers in his own conduct, for children are not indifferent to what they see in others, and they much sooner copy evil than good examples: they certainly take notice of all our movements, and consequently the greatest caution is necessary. It would be of little purpose to endeavour to inculcate suitable precepts in the minds of the children, unless they were to see them shine forth in the conduct of the teacher. I shall not easily forget, "*Please, sir, you stole my whistle!*"

How awkward it would sound, if, when a teacher was explaining to his pupils the sin of swearing, a child was to say, "Please, Sir, I heard you swear."

Persons who have charge of children cannot be too circumspect, and certain it is, their character can never be too good, as every trifling fault will be magnified both by parents and children. Indeed the character of a person who has the charge of children is of so much importance, that very often the designs of benevolent persons are frustrated by appointing improper persons to fill such situations. Patience is absolutely indispensable, as it will frequently take the master or mistress, a whole hour to investigate into a subject that may appear of little or no importance; such as one child accusing another of stealing some trifling thing, as a plum, a cherry, a button, or some such thing. The complainant and defendant will expect justice done to them by the master or mistress, and in order to do this, much time and trouble will, in some cases, be necessary

Should a hasty conclusion be formed, and the accused be punished for what he has not been guilty of, in such case the child will be sensible that an injury has been done to him, and will feel dissatisfied with his tutors, and consequently will not pay them that respect they ought to have; besides, it will frequently be found, on examination, that the accuser is really the most in fault, and I think I have convinced many children that this has been the case, and they have retired satisfied with my decision; for when a child is satisfied that justice will be done to him, he will open his case freely and boldly, but if he has any idea that justice will not be done to him, why then he will keep one half the facts of the case in his own mind, and will not care to reveal them. I once formed a hasty conclusion in the case of two children, and happened to decide the very reverse to what I ought to have done; the consequence was, that the child endeavoured to do that for himself, which he found I had not done for him, and pleaded his own cause with the opposite party in the play-ground; but finding that he could not prevail on him, and being sensible that he had been wronged, he was so much hurt, that he brought his father the next day, and we re-considered the case; when it was found, that the child was correct, and that I had decided wrong. Here I found how necessary it was to exercise the utmost patience, in order to enable me to judge right, and to convince my little pupils, that I had the greatest desire to do them justice. I compare an Infant School to a little commonwealth, or a world in miniature, the head or governor of which, in a natural point of view, is the master. He will have to act the part of counsel, judge, and jury, and although the children cannot find words to plead their own cause, yet by their looks and gestures, they will convince you that they have some internal evidence that you have decided right; and it appears to me, that the future conduct of the children in the world, will depend, in a great measure, upon the correctness of the master's decision. One would suppose, to hear the observations of some persons, that mere automatons would do for masters and mistresses. By such persons the system is considered as every thing, while the persons who are to teach it, have been considered as secondary objects; but it strikes me, that a system, however perfect in itself, will prove nearly abortive, unless it is committed to persons possessed of some degree of skill. We cannot be too circumspect in the choice of persons unto whom we commit the care and education of the rising generation, for there is something so powerful in virtue and correctness of deportment, that even infants respect it; and this will operate more powerfully on their minds, than many are aware of, for we cannot help respecting virtue, wherever we find it; but vice is detestable at all times. It does not appear necessary to me, to keep children at such an immense distance from their tutors; they should rather be encouraged to make their tutor their confident, for by this means he will become acquainted with many things that will prove both useful to him and them; but should the child be kept at so great a distance, he will seek some other persons to whom he may open his little mind, and should that person be ill disposed, the most serious consequences will not unfrequently follow. Let it not be supposed, however, that I am vain enough to believe that I am in possession of the qualifications I have been recommending, for we must all be prepared to fall short of what we aim at; but I trust, I know the source from whence all assistance is derived, and I am taught to believe, that such assistance will not be withheld from those who diligently seek it. I am well aware, that I shall have to render an account of my stewardship to the Almighty, for every child that may have been placed under my care, and indeed, I feel that it requires much assistance from above—

"To rear the tender thought;
To teach the young idea how to shoot;
To pour the fresh instruction o'er the mind;
To breathe th' enlivening spirit; and to fix
The generous purpose in the glowing breast."

Let not those, then, who are similarly circumstanced with myself, think that I address them in the spirit of arrogance, with a preconceived opinion of my own sufficiency. I hope that all who teach may be more fit for the situation than I am. I know many who are an honor to their profession, as well as the situation they fill, but I am sorry to say, that I think they do not all meet with the encouragement they merit. It is not always those who do their duty the best, that meet with the most encouragement: but there is one thing to be said, if a man's conscience does not upbraid him, he need not care what the world thinks of him, for conscience is a faithful monitor, and will seldom deceive us, if we attend to its dictates.

If abilities be necessary to manage children from eight to fourteen years of age, they are equally so for the management of infants from eighteen months to seven years, and I am inclined to think, from what I have seen and experienced, that the success of an institution of this kind, will depend very much on the conduct and ability of those to whom it is entrusted. If any one qualification, therefore, is more necessary than another, in those who have charge of an infant school, it is, as observed in *The Teacher's Magazine,* " Piety."—" *Seek first the kingdom of God and his righteousness, and all these things will be added unto you.*"

Questions and Answers concerning the Geometrical Figures.

WE will suppose there is a pasteboard against the wall, and the children standing round it in a semicircle; the teacher being provided with a pointer, (the same as is used for the pictures), he will put the following questions, pointing to an equilateral triangle.

Q. What is this?
A. An Equilateral Triangle.
Q. Why is it called an Equilateral Triangle.
A. Because its sides are all equal.
Q. How many sides has it?
A. Three sides.
Q. How many angles has it?
A. Three angles.
Q. What do you mean by the angles?
A. The corners.

Q. What do you mean by equal.
A. When the three sides are like each other.

Isoceles Triangle.

Q. What is this?
A. An acute angled Isoceles Triangle.
Q. What does acute mean.
A. When the angles are sharp.
Q. Why is it called an Isoceles Triangle?
A. Because only two of its sides are equal.
Q. How many sides has it?
A. Three, the same as the other.
Q. Are there any other kind of Isoceles Triangles?
A. Yes, there is right angled and obtuse angled.

Here the pointer is to be put to the other triangles, and the master must explain to the children the meaning of right angled and obtuse angled.

Scalene Triangle.

Q. What is this?
A. An acute angled Scalene Triangle.
Q. Why is it called an acute angled Scalene Triangle.

A. Because the corners are sharp and none of its sides are equal.

Q. Are there any other kind of Scalene Triangles?

A. Yes, there is a right angled Scalene Triangle.

Q. What else?

A. An obtuse angled Scalene Triangle.

Q. Can an acute Triangle be an Equilateral Triangle?

A. Yes, it may be Equilateral, Isoceles, or Scalene.

Q. Can a right angled Triangle, or an obtuse angled Triangle, be an Equilateral?

A. No, it must either be an Isoceles or a Scalene Triangle.

Square.

Q. What is this?

A. A square.

Q. Why is it called a square?

A. Because all its angles are right angles, and its sides are equal.

Q. How many angles has it?

A. Four angles.

Q. What would it make if we draw a line from one angle to the opposite one?

A. Two right angled Isoceles Triangles.

Q. What would you call the line that we drew from one angle to the other?
A. A diagonal.
Q. Suppose we draw another line from the other two angles.
A. Then it would make four Triangles.

Pentagon.

Q. What is this?
A. A regular Pentagon.
Q. Why is it called a Pentagon?
A. Because it has five sides and five angles.
Q. Why is it called regular?
A. Because its sides and angles are equal.
Q. What does Pentagon mean?
A. A five sided figure.
Q. Are there any other kinds of Pentagons?
A. Yes, irregular Pentagons.
Q. What does irregular mean?
A. When the sides and angles are not equal.

Hexagons.

Q. What is this?
A. An Hexagon.

Q. Why is it called an Hexagon?
A. Because it has six sides and six angles.
Q. What does Hexagon mean?
A. A six-sided figure.
Q. Is there more than one sort of Hexagons?
A. Yes, there is regular and irregular.
Q. What is a regular Hexagon?
A. When the sides and angles are all equal.
Q. What is an irregular Hexagon?
A. When the sides and angles are not equal.

Heptagon.

Q. What is this?
A. A regular Heptagon.
Q. Why is it called an Heptagon?
A. Because it has seven sides and seven angles.
Q. Why is it called a regular Heptagon.
A. Because its sides and angles are equal.
Q. What does an Heptagon mean?
A. A seven-sided figure.
Q. What is an irregular Heptagon?
A. A seven-sided figure, whose sides are not equal.

Octagon.

Q. What is this?
A. A regular Octagon.
Q. Why is it called a regular Octagon?
A. Because it has eight sides and eight angles.
Q. What does an Octagon mean?
A. An eight-sided figure.
Q. What is an irregular Octagon?
A. An eight-sided figure, whose sides and angles are not equal.
Q. What does an octave mean?
A. Eight notes in music.

Nonagon.

Q. What is this?
A. A regular Nonagon.
Q. Why is it called a Nonagon?
A. Because it has nine sides and nine angles?
Q. What does a Nonagon mean?
A. A nine-sided figure.
Q. What is an irregular Nonagon?
A. A nine-sided figure, whose sides and angles are not equal.

Decagon.

Q. What is this?
A. A regular Decagon.
Q. What does a Decagon mean?
A. A ten-sided figure.
Q. Why is it called a Decagon?
A. Because it has ten sides and ten angles, and there are both regular and irregular Decagons.

The other polygons are taught the children in rotation, in the same simple manner, all tending to please and edify them. They are taught the principle of brick-building, by wood blocks, made the proper size, so that they may build the front of a house, walls, &c. They may also be taught the principle, in some degree, by which bridges are built, and we have children who can spring an arch, and tell the names of the things connected with it; in short, there is no end of teaching children, if we so simplify the things that they can comprehend them. Perhaps it may be thought that I am going into the opposite extreme in attempting to teach infants these things; but if any person doubts the possibility of infants being taught them, they can satisfy themselves by calling at the school; and I once more beg leave to remark, that variety forms the most pleasant food for the human mind.

Conclusion.

IF a person has not been fortunate enough to receive what the world calls a good education, if he yet possesses piety, he will be assisted by his heavenly Father where he is deficient; accordingly, we find that many of the disciples of our Lord were fishermen. We do not look among this description of persons for literature, and what the world calls learning; and yet, it cannot be denied, they exhibited talents of no mean cast, and were gifted, by their divine Master, with such abilities as fitted them for the work he intended they should do. "How mysterious are thy ways O God, who was ever disappointed that asked of thee in a right spirit?" Prosper thy work which is begun in the world, we beseech thee, O Lord; may thy gracious providence so encircle and protect the rising generation, that there may be no more complaining in our streets. Protect them, O Lord, from the many dangers that surround them, as soon as they draw their breath in this vale of tears, and put into the hearts of those who have the means, to consider the state of the infant poor, and to give them the assistance they need. Grant that thy blessed example may be followed by many, for thou didst desire that children should come unto thee, and not be forbidden, and thou didst take them up in thine arms and bless them, declaring that of such is the kingdom of heaven. May thy creatures therefore not be ashamed to notice little children, but co-operate hand and heart with each other, and endeavour to teach them all good. May thy divine hand be seen in that glorious institution "*The Bible Society*," where men of various opinions are joined together, to forward the blessed work, which thou hast begun; so may they also join hand and heart in endeavouring to rescue the infant race from danger; that so these tender plants may be nurtured with the dew of thy divine blessing, and thus made fit subjects for thy heavenly kingdom, where the wicked cease from troubling, and the weary are at rest. May thy divine influence descend abundantly upon all those who have hitherto turned their attention to infant children; may they feel great pleasure in doing good; may they receive thy grace and protection abundantly, and when their days of probation are ended, may they find a place in thy heavenly mansions, and there glorify thee throughout the boundless ages of eternity. Amen.

APPENDIX.

Reply to Dr. Pole's strictures, and those of the Edinburgh Review, on the Author's mode of punishment, and the adopting of prayer and praise in Infant Schools.

THE general utility of coporeal punishment, when it shall be found necessary, appears to me to be justified both by Scripture and experience, and consequently, that teachers must either have recourse to it, or expel refractory children from their schools. Now, I ask, which is the best, to expel a child, and thereby deprive it of the benefit of instruction, or to have recourse to slight coporeal punishment? If children are to be allowed to do as they please, and the whole system is to consist in mere amusement, (as stated in the Edinburgh Review, for May, 1823, page 448), then I admit that coporeal punishment may be unnecessary; but I never understood, that the system was to consist in amusement merely, I had always thought, before I had read this document, that education and amusement were to be combined.

I beg leave, therefore, to notice some of the remarks which have been made against one or two particulars in my system. The punishment which I stated that I occasionally adopted, was, that when all other plans had failed, I gave the offender a slight tap with a small twig on the hand. Dr. Pole observes, that "no such instrument of correction should ever be admitted into these schools, that our own tempers, under much provocation, are not always to be trusted." But if this instrument is to be prohibited, and our own tempers not to be trusted, what is to prevent us from lifting up our hand, and giving a child a box on the ear; and is it not better to permit a lesser evil to prevent a greater? No one, surely, will assert, that a box on the ear is less objectionable than a slight pat on the hand.

I beg to add, that I have dispensed with the cage and green baize, not from a conviction of their barbarity or absurdity, but from a desire to prevent controversy, and to unite in endeavouring to form a system fit for general adoption. A slight tap on the hand appears to me to be far preferable to handcuffs and stocks, as used in the Bristol school. I am sure they never saw those things adopted at the parent institution. To prove that my system has not been marked by severity, I may remark, that, during the months of June and July, 1823, there was upwards of fifty persons applied to have their children admitted, all of whom we were obliged to refuse, so that my remarks, on the ground of experience with this class of children, will go as far as those of my opponents. From the time I commenced my duty down to the present time, I have had eight hundred and sixty-six children pass through my hands, which may be seen by reference to the books that are kept for the purpose, and some of the children that have been sent to other schools, are now in the highest class, who can read and write as well as I can. We are told by the Edinburgh Review, that the best way to cure a quarrelsome and refractory child, is to take him on the knee and reason with him. What effect reasoning will have upon children, at the tender age they are admitted into an infant school, I will not pretend to determine, especially when they are in a passion. We know that few men will pay much attention to reason, when they are in a passion; still less can we expect it from young children. However, we are told, this is an infallible rule to go by, and that it is only necessary to be known, to become generally adopted. I must confess that punishing a child is the most disagreeable part of one's duty, and will be viewed as such by all persons with the least spark of humanity; and feeling this to be the case, I eagerly caught at any plan that promised to ease me of so much trouble; and I soon had an opportunity of putting the plan into practice. A certain child, who manifested an early disposition to bear rule over the other children, gave one of them a blow on the nose, which caused it to bleed much, and, as far as I could learn from the little witnesses, for no other reason than because the child would not let the culprit make a horse of him, and ride him about the play-ground at pleasure. The children reasoned with him, in their way, and told him that it was wrong to fight his schoolfellows, and afterwards informed me of the circumstance; but two of them met with a similar fate for telling me. The offender had only been in the school three days. To have seen the three children, with their noses bleeding, and the alarm that was depicted in the countenances of the others, one would have thought that some wild beast had got in amongst them. My wife took the three children, to wash their faces, while I took the culprit on my knee, to reason with him, as directed. I had scarcely spoken two words, before he applied his hand to my face. I was determined to give the plan a fair trial, and merely called him a naughty boy for striking me; he immediately gave me another blow: "Oh," exclaimed the other children, "see how he is hitting master in the face." "So I will," says the offender." As to getting the three children to kiss the offender, it was not possible, for they would not come within a yard of him. It was impossible not to perceive, that either him or I must be master, and I was fearful, if I suffered it to pass unpunished, that some of the other children would soon begin to take the same liberty, and that I might become a mere cypher amongst them. Being at a loss how to proceed, and finding myself foiled in the first attempt, I was obliged to have recourse to the objected method, and accordingly gave him two pats on the hand; for which, in return, he gave me several kicks on the legs; I then favoured him with the punishment of carrying the broom on his shoulder, and made him carry it round the school as long as I thought proper; however, he soon began to exhibit symptoms of tameness, and let me do any thing that I pleased with him afterwards. I am not aware that he has ever struck a child since, and I am certain he has never struck me, and I have no more trouble with him now than I have with any of the others; so that we see, although this is violence opposed to violence, and is not proceeding upon a rational principle, (according to the extract in the Edinburgh Review) yet we find it produces a radical amendment, when that which they recommend **totally failed**. I do not mean to say that the method recommended will not do in some cases, but we see that it will not do in all; so that we come to this conclusion, "that whatever is best administered, (in these cases) is best." We are told in the next place, "that we are to get the contending parties to kiss each other, and make them walk round the school, with their arms round each other's necks;" and we are further informed, that this is a far more likely method* than that which I pursue. With respect to their walking round the school, hand in hand, I have not the least objection to, but I think it is carrying the thing too far, to make them kiss each other. If the children choose to do it of their own accord, it may be well, providing they are both of one sex, but I cannot see any utility in insisting upon their doing it, especially if the offenders are above six years of age, and should happen to be one of each sex. It may not only be disorderly, after this age, but improper, inasmuch as we cannot expect that the internal feelings will correspond with the external

---

* I am glad to hear that this method is so successful in a certain quarter, but I really have so much to do in minding my own concerns, that I cannot spare time to find fault with the inventions of others.

act. Besides, children are quite forward enough in these particulars, without having any additional stimulus.

Let us suppose a child plays the truant; he is sent to school by his parents, but chuses to disobey their orders, tramples both upon their's and the master's authority. If this child went to the Bristol school, according to their own account, they would put the stocks on his legs; if he belonged to the Spitalfields infant school, he would have a pat on the hand, or probably have to carry one of the brooms round the school. We don't want any extra machine for punishing the children; the same broom that sweeps the school will do for us. Let us further suppose, that the method adopted at the former place had the desired effect, and that my method was as successful, (which I have found it to be) the consequence would be, that the child would be afraid to stay away from the former institution, for fear of having the stocks put on his legs,* and he would be afraid to stay away from the latter institution, for fear of having to carry the broom. This is really finding fault without reason, for the principle is exactly the same in both cases. I can see no more cruelty in one than in the other;

* The master says that this is considered a most ignominious punishment, amongst the children, and I certainly do admire the children's taste.

K

but if there is any difference between the two methods, I must say, as a father, that I should prefer the latter; not because it is my method, but because it does not appear so degrading, nor savour so much of prison discipline as the former. The writer in the Edinburgh Review goes on to state, " who indeed, that had ever reflected on the first outlines even of the plan, could ever dream of punishing the children for playing the truant, when the whole system consists in making the school a place of amusement, and the best proof of your having failed in pursuing it is the necessity of compelling the children, by fear, to give their attendance." In the first place, I am at a loss to conceive what system this writer speaks of, and can but regret that it was never published and given in detail. If he means the system, or plan, that is adopted at Bristol, it was impossible for me to pursue it, for the Spitalfields school was established prior to it; if he means the system that is adopted at the parent institution, I can assure him that the master of that institution taught me no such plan as he describes, for he expressly told me that the plan did not consist in mere amusement, for that it was expected that every child was to be taught a lesson in the alphabet, spelling, &c. every day.

Who indeed that ever had the least practice with children would dream of letting them play the truant, and not take any notice of it; but let them come in and out of the school at all hours, just as they please; stay away when they like, and come when they like. If this is the plan that is to be pursued, I take upon me to say it will not answer. How can we expect to reform the character, if children are allowed to do as they please. I do not wonder at parents not sending their children, if this is the case, for how do they know but that their children may be brought home crippled, or lifeless, by being run over, while they had imagined their children were safe at school. The poor are not so beside themselves, as not to see the fallacy of a plan of this description; indeed there can be no need to say more on this subject, as it speaks for itself. But it is further stated in the same publication, that "the best proof of your having failed in pursuing this system, is the necessity of compelling the children, by fear, to give their attendance." If children were perfect beings, there might be no necessity for compelling them to attend school; for they would see their own interest in attending; but alas, we are all too apt to stray from the correct path; we do not always attend to such counsel, and at such places, as would prove most beneficial to us, and the reason of this is, that by nature we are inclined to evil, and were it not for the divine providence, the best of us would rush into every kind of danger. Children very early manifest the same dispositions, and let me ask by what method are we to counteract these dispositions, but by forcing those, who would stay away, to give their attendance. Is it not supposed that children attend school for the purpose of being taught what is good, and to have their bad principles eradicated? and can any time be more proper, or more likely to prove successful, than the first stages of infancy? If the pasture is ever so good, there will always be some sheep stray from the flock, and it appears to me to be a duty to pay a particular attention to those sheep that are likely to stray: nay, this appears to be the chief end and design of all schools. I cannot perceive that I have failed in pursuing a rational system; but should any better system be pointed out, founded on experience, and agreeable to right reason, I shall feel most happy (if permitted) to adopt it. I have not taken up my opinion lightly; I have strong grounds for what I have advanced: but if any real improvement can be shown that will tend to the good of society, and the good of the children, it shall meet with attention; but I cannot perceive what good it would be to the children, to suffer them to stay away from school whenever they please. It is not so easy a thing to break a child of bad habits, as some persons imagine; the mere "standing a child in the school, with a placard denoting his offence," (as recommended) will not always succeed. Our plans must be various, and suited to the disposition of the child. What will cure one child may not cure another; this must be known to every person who has had any practice with children. Much has been said about my subjecting offenders to ridicule, but it would seem, that there can be very little difference between " standing a child in a school, with a placard suspended to it" for all the other children to see, or causing it to walk round the school, with the broom on its shoulder. In the latter case the business is performed in the space of two minutes, for when the child has walked once or twice round the school, and begins to manifest some degree of repentance, the punishment is over, and the child resumes his station in the school; but, in the former case, it will take much longer time, and a child that had been accustomed to wear the placard, and stand in the way proposed, would think it no punishment at all, and soon begin to care little or nothing about it; and I think that punishment which is soonest over is preferable.

I shall now add a few remarks as to singing and prayer in infant schools. Dr. Pole objects to both singing and prayer in infant schools, and assigns as a reason for so doing, that " it is possible the gratification of the creature may be more consulted than the will of the Creator." This certainly has great weight, and I fear is but too tue, in many cases, when applied to adults, and I confess I have profited by the hint; but it does not follow, that because a thing is liable to abuse, that it should be discontinued altogether. As well might we object to public worship, because hypocrites are found assembled with real worshippers. It will be seen then, that I admit the full force of Dr. Pole's remarks, when applied to adults; but I cannot perceive that they apply with equal force to infants, who may be taught, I think, to praise God from the heart, and in genuine simplicity. Let it be observed, that the prayer and praise which is offered up to the Deity in a state of humility, is most likely to be acceptable, and the infant state is certainly the most humble; it was for this reason that our Lord Jesus Christ said, " suffer little children to come unto me, and forbid them not, for of such is the kingdom of heaven." We may plainly infer from this, that if we praise and pray in a state of humility, it is most likely to prove acceptable to the Creator and profitable to the creature; and I am confirmed in this opinion, by viewing the countenances of my little scholars, when they are performing this duty; it often appears that their very souls are employed in the work; and as far as I am concerned, I may truly say, that I have frequently felt such a powerful influence decending from above, that I cannot find words to describe, which has forcibly reminded me of a passage in scripture,—" Out of the mouths of babes and sucklings thou hast perfected praise." Several ladies have told me, that they thought they had never witnessed genuine praise before, and one gentleman in particular was so much impressed with what he had heard and seen, that he wrote down his thoughts on the spot, the tears trickling down his cheeks while he was writing, and left me the following document, wishing it might be painted on a board, and hung up in the school; " Let no person depart from this school, without presenting a fervent petition to the Most High, for a blessing upon the Institution." There were eight visitors present at the time, and among them, a person who was in training for an Infant School at Liverpool, and is now, I believe, the master of that institution, who can confirm what is here written. It appears to me that praise and prayer are inseparably connected together, and that we cannot, with propriety, dispense with either; and if more proof were necessary, it might be abundantly supplied from the Scriptures.

Praise and prayer operate as connecting mediums between man and the Creator. Prayer to God is the duty of all men; we live, move, and have our being in Him. Every good and perfect gift proceeds from

Him: men ought therefore to pray and not faint: we are so sinful, that we always need mercy; so weak that we always need help; so empty, that we always need fresh supplies; so exposed that we always need protection; and, I think, we should be somewhat cautious in condemning these things, when we perceive what dependent beings we are. Besides, prayer is commanded by Jesus Christ himself, "After this manner, therefore, pray ye." I know of no better prayer than that which is taught in the gospel, known by the name of the Lord's Prayer; this comprehends all we can ask, and all we are capable of receiving; so that I can see no harm in teaching children this prayer, but on the contrary much good is likely to accrue from it. However, I am fully aware, that it is possible to get into the opposite extreme, by having these things done at improper times, and particularly prayer. There is a straight path to pursue, and if a man is willing to be guided by reason and revelation, it is most likely that he will be led into it. I only offer my opinion, which every man has a right to do; and at the same time, I trust, to pay proper respect to the opinions of others; yet, however desirous I may be to listen to the arguments of my superiors, I cannot give up a point, that is in my view, of the first importance, namely, praying to, and " praising the Creator in the days of our youth."

Not that I would be understood to insinuate that no good may be done in schools, where these two things are not adopted, but what I mean to say, is, that more good will be done to both parents and children, by the performance of them, at proper times, than by excluding them altogether; both praise and prayer are adopted in the Spitalfields Infant School, and the parents and children have no reason to regret; thus it may be proper to state, that the children repeat their prayers once in the morning, and once in the afternoon, which is always the first thing they do, and the children always kneel while they are repeating it. Prayer is not considered a mere school exercise, but a paramount duty, which the children, in conjunction with all other human beings, are bound to perform: those who can do without prayer must be somewhat superior to human beings. Agesilaus being asked what he thought most proper for boys to learn, answered, "what they ought to do when they become men."

𝔉𝔦𝔫𝔦𝔰.

The following Extracts from the different Reviews, are inserted as testimonials of the first Edition:

"WE have no space to enter upon the subject of early Juvenile delinquency, to the consideration of which, Mr. Wilderspin's book naturally invites us, and for the prevention of which, Infant Schools seem to present a more hopeful remedy, than most other plans which have been suggested. Our author shall relate, in his own way, one of his adventures, in his benevolent rambles, which will furnish a good commentary on all that has been stated both in and out of parliament, on this great moral and national question."

Christian Observer, May, 1823.

"We cordially approve of the plan, particularly as due care seems to be taken for the exercise, amusement, and health of the little pupils; and we hope a cheap edition of this book will be printed, for circulation through the country, whereby it may prove a national benefit."

Evangelical Magazine, April, 1823.

"We found it impossible to lay the book down until we had read the whole, and were in consequence, induced to take the earliest opportunity of visiting the School, a visit which afforded the highest gratification."

Christian Guardian, April, 1823.

"We cannot conclude our remarks, without returning thanks to Mr. W. for this interesting and useful, though plain and unadorned volume, and we sincerely recommend all our readers to procure it for their own use, and should they be heads of families, we may add, that there are, throughout, many valuable hints, founded on experience, which deserve the serious attention of every parent."

Teacher's Magazine, February, 1823.

"We have read this little book with uncommon pleasure.—Infant Schools, under religious and judicious management, would be an inestimable blessing, in every considerable town and village of the kingdom.

"All who feel it a duty to preserve their generation, are, we think, bound in conscience to encourage and extend this new and most important scheme for the prevention of Juvenile delinquency, and for the promotion of the best interests of Society."

Wesleyan Methodists' Magazine, for April, 1823.

"We clearly gather, from the information which Mr. W. gives us, that similar schools must be of essential service to the labouring classes in every part of the kingdom; and that, as is well observed by Mr. Lloyd, who writes the preface, they are particularly needed in manufacturing districts."

Inquirer, April, 1823, *page* 345.

Erratum: Page 66. line 5.—*for* City—*read* Country

Goyder, Printer, 415, Strand

www.ingramcontent.com/pod-product-compliance
Lightning Source LLC
Chambersburg PA
CBHW080435110426
42743CB00016B/3175